Growing Up in the Cooper Country

Growing Up in the Cooper Country

BOYHOOD RECOLLECTIONS OF
THE NEW YORK FRONTIER

Edited by
LOUIS C. JONES

SYRACUSE UNIVERSITY PRESS 1965

Contents

Introduction

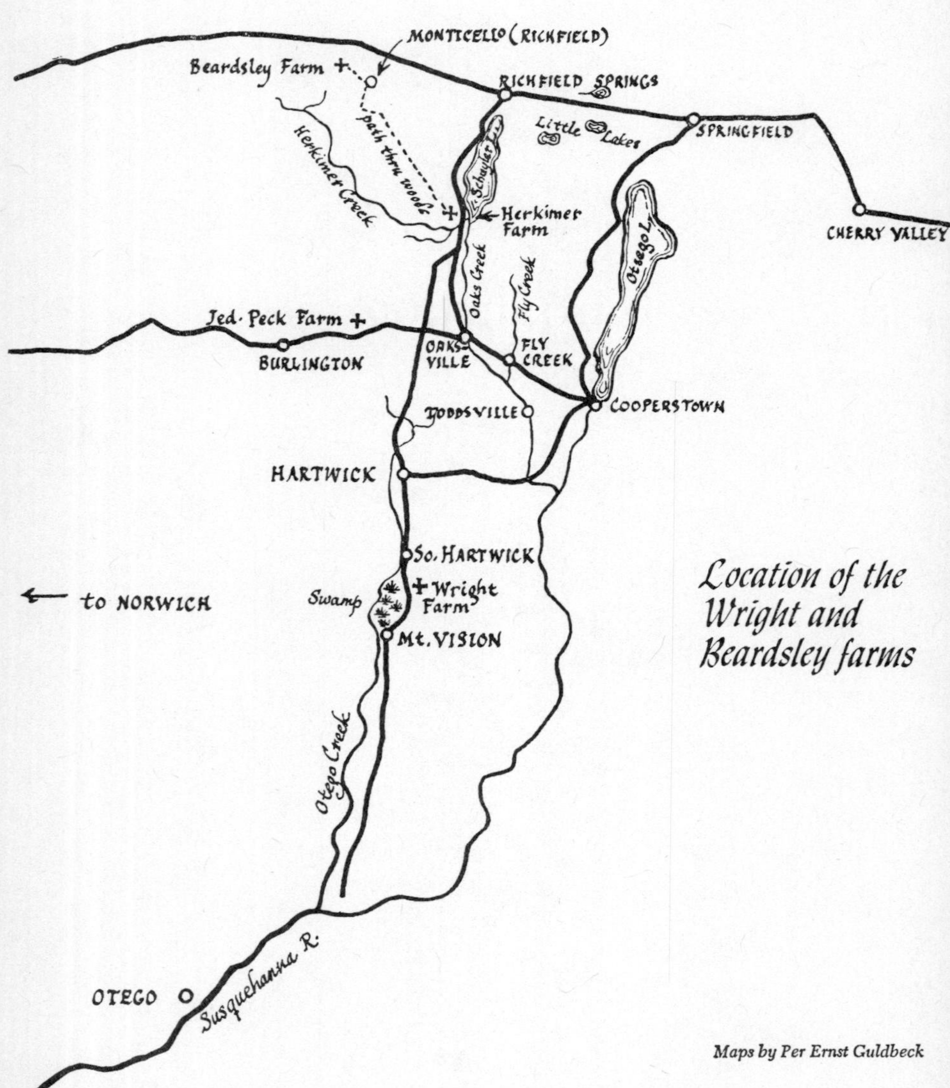

MONTICELLO (RICKFIELD)
Beardsley Farm
RICHFIELD SPRINGS
Little Lakes
SPRINGFIELD
path thru woods
Herkimer Creek
Schuyler L.
Herkimer Farm
Oaks Creek
Fly Creek
Otsego L.
CHERRY VALLEY
Jed. Peck Farm
BURLINGTON
OAKS-VILLE
FLY CREEK
TODDSVILLE
COOPERSTOWN
HARTWICK
So. HARTWICK
to NORWICH
Swamp
Wright Farm
Mt. VISION
Otego Creek
Susquehanna R.
OTEGO
Location of the Wright and Beardsley farms
Maps by Per Ernst Guldbeck

June 16, 1806, had been anticipated in Otsego County, New York, with great excitement ever since the publication of *Phinney's Almanac* for 1806 had announced that there would be a total eclipse of the sun on that date. Mr. Phinney, who also published the *Otsego Herald*, described the phenomenon in his issue of June 19. The atmosphere was serene and the sun majestically bright until 9:50 a.m., when the eclipse began. By quarter past ten the stars were out, and an hour later the sun was completely obscured. Fowls retired to their nests, and only the whippoorwill was heard in the forest. Then, slowly but wondrously, the sun returned and it was day again.

For thousands who saw this phenomenon it must have remained, always, an exciting memory. At least two of Mr. Phinney's younger readers in Otsego County never forgot. In 1806 Levi Beardsley was a young buck of twenty-one, who later recorded in his *Reminiscences* that he was working that day on the family farm near Richfield Springs. Eighteen miles south, as the crow flies, a nine-year-old boy, Henry Clarke Wright, was hoeing corn that same morning; nearly half a century later he, too, would record the event and its impressions on his sensitive mind in his autobiography, *Human Life*.

These two young pioneers represented the first and second waves of immigration to the New York frontier following the Revolution, when, suddenly, New England and the Hudson Valley burst out of their bounds and overflowed into a wilderness at long last free of the threat of Indians. Beardsley, at the time a boy of five, came with his family in 1790; Wright's people came a full decade later, when little Henry was a three-year-old. Those ten years between 1790 and 1800 had seen the population of Otsego County, 70 miles west of Albany, increase nine times from an estimated 2,420 to 21,636; they had seen a thousand square miles of virtually unbroken forest become spotted with clearings. Cooperstown, the county seat, had become a thriving village of three hundred souls. When the Beardsleys arrived they cleared their own land of trees, but Wright's father was able to buy a farmhouse already constructed, although such purchases must still have been rare.

These two boys, unknown to each other, growing up nearby and under very similar circumstances, born of parents of much the same background, were to head, one for the law, the other for the pulpit; Beardsley was to become a successful, highly regarded legislator and politician, while Wright was to be both beloved and reviled as a radical, abolitionist, pacifist, and educational reformer. It is our good fortune that both of these men wrote autobiographies; Henry Clarke Wright's *Human Life* was published in 1849, when he was fifty-two, and Levi Beardsley's *Reminiscences* came out in 1852, when the author was sixty-seven. They both devoted a considerable portion of their work to accounts of their youth, so that between them we get a comprehensive and doubly verified view of what it was like to be a boy on the New York frontier.

This present volume has excerpted from the two books those sections descriptive of their youth; the result is a boy's-eye view of rural life on the New York frontier from 1790 to about 1817—work, play, school, church, militia, dances, conversions, bear hunts, and all the rest of it, as two men of very different points of view remembered it. The juxtaposing of these two boyhood accounts has seemed worth while because, while the locales and the times are almost identical, the two writers are so different that the overall images are quite different. Wright is critical of practically every aspect of the social pattern he knew as a boy—religion, education, sports, drinking, smoking. Beardsley says very little about either education or religion, much about politics, militia, bear hunts, clearing the forest, the pleasures of life; he enjoyed and excelled at all the sports and continued to hunt all his life. Tobacco and alcohol were sensible adjuncts to life and it never occurred to him to reject them.

The country to which their parents had brought them was a hilly, reasonably fertile water-rich woodland that had been opened up to settlers by William Cooper in 1786. Cooper is one of the neglected architects of the New York frontier and one of its more colorful characters. It is unfortunate that this vigorous, wise leader of pioneers should have been reduced to footnotes in the biographies of his novelist son, James Fenimore Cooper. One of the most useful keys to an understanding of the forest he opened up to settlement is his little volume of letters, called *A Guide in the Wilderness*. Here a man who had settled 40,000 souls on his own land, who had encouraged the "poorest order of men" to buy their acres on an installment plan, tells how it was done, how land was best selected, how cleared and planted; he writes of the wildlife, the values of maple syrup and ashes as first crops, the problems of founding a small community.

Cooper was a Federalist and a rough-and-tumble politician; the fight with Cochran recounted by Beardsley was not his only fracas; indeed, his death in 1809 came from a blow on the back of the head after a political meeting in

Albany. He moves in and out of the Beardsley narrative as a figure of distinction, the first county judge, first Member of Congress, performing the first marriage, securing the appointment of Obadiah Beardsley as a justice of the peace. His great virtue lay in his confidence and trust in men of no means, when his own social peers, his political allies, like the Van Rensselaers and the Livingstons and his lawyer, Alexander Hamilton, were dubious and fearful. He understood men better than they.

In a day when the great landlords were reasserting the importance of leasing rather than selling farmsteads, William Cooper wrote: "The poor man, and his class is most numerous, will generally undertake about one hundred acres. The best mode of dealing with him is to grant him the fee-simple by deed, and secure the purchase money by a mortgage on the land conveyed to him. He then feels himself, if I may use the phrase, as a man upon record. His views extend themselves to his posterity, and he contemplates with pleasure their settlement on the estate he has created, a sentiment ever grateful to the heart of man; his spirit is enlivened, his industry is quickened, every new object he attains brings a new ray of hope and courage; he builds himself a barn and a better habitation, plants his fruit trees, and lays out his garden; he clears away the trees, until they, which were the first obstacles to his improvement, becoming scarcer, become more valuable, and he is at length as anxious to preserve as he was at first to destroy them; he no longer feels the weight of debt, for having the fee he can sell at an improved value, nor is he bound against his will."

Someone has said of William Cooper that he was a mixture of silk hose and leather stocking and this is very sound. When his son came to describe him in *The Pioneers* (as Judge Templeton), his urbanity, his social graces, his kindness came out more clearly than his sympathy with his horny-handed neighbors. The novelist remembered the domestic figure; Beardsley remembered the public figure. James Fenimore Cooper was only four years younger than Levi Beardsley and while one of them was growing up in Otsego Hall, the noblest mansion west of Albany, the other was living in a log house a few miles to the north. The men and women described by both Beardsley and Wright were the farmers and craftsmen who had been encouraged to come into the wilderness by the senior Cooper. Neither the Wrights nor the Beardsleys happened to live on Cooper lands, but these were only the accidents of real estate transactions; they were of the same breed of men.

William Cooper's *A Guide in the Wilderness* is written in a clear, vigorous eighteenth-century style that would do honor to Addison; if James Fenimore Cooper's *The Pioneers* is stylistically less palatable, nevertheless it provides an invaluable background for Beardsley and Wright. Again, this novel draws on the memory of a grown man depicting the world of his boyhood. It is, geographically, the same world but viewed from the mansion rather than the farmhouse. It reflects an upper class distance from the folk life which neither of the other men ever reached. James Fenimore Cooper was always the son of the 'Squire, the Congressman, the Judge, while Beardsley and Wright took equal pride in their muddied boots and homely backgrounds.

The Pioneers, however, has memorable scenes that elucidate our two writers. The fishing scene, the hunting of passenger pigeons, the turkey shoot, the descriptions of burning and clearing the land, the beginnings of the church and a dozen other passages are all of a piece with the *Reminiscences* and *Human Life*. But Cooper himself is always above and apart in a way that was not characteristic of his father or his two contemporaries. As for his firsthand knowledge of Indians, it was probably not very different from Wright's, whose touching account of a visit from an Indian family is echoed in many accounts of family folklore in central New York in the early nineteenth century.

Levi Beardsley, son of Obadiah, grandson of another Obadiah, was born in Hoosick, New York, on November 13, 1785, on his ancestral farm which formed a part of the *mise en scène* for the Battle of Bennington. It is irritating —but necessary—to point out that this skirmish, which so greatly influenced the crucial battle of Saratoga, took place on New York soil, although one never could find a Vermonter to admit it. (New Englanders can never get over the curious misconception that the American Revolution is their own private property.) Grandfather Obadiah, who was fifty at the time of the battle (1777), was no enthusiastic patriot, influenced perhaps by his brother John, an Episcopal clergyman who once had preached before the King. While Obadiah may have been well disposed toward his brother's monarch, he had no intention of having his log house become a key to the Hessian and Indian strategy during the battle. When a Hessian soldier began knocking the chinks out from between his log walls, so that he could aim through them, Grandfather seized the musket, tossed it into a back room and tossed the Hessian out the door. This was but a token of what was soon to happen to the Hessian's colleagues; their Indian allies ran off through the brush and they retreated, leaving the crucial American supplies intact, to be used two months later at Saratoga.

The Beardsleys had already been in this country 138 years by that time, having come from Stratford-on-Avon to Stratford, Connecticut, in 1639. In Levi's grandfather's generation they had first moved to Dutchess County, New

York, thence to Hoosick in Rensselaer County. Levi's father, Obadiah, was born in 1763 and so was twenty-seven when the family moved west to the Otsego country. Levi's mother, Eunice Moore, came of active Dutch stock from Long Island and New Jersey, Baptists and strongly revolutionary Whigs. By 1790 Obadiah and Eunice had three children: Levi, born on November 13, 1785; a two-year-old daughter; and a new baby, Samuel, destined to a career even more distinguished than Levi's; he would become a Congressman and Chief Justice of the State Supreme Court.

The Beardsleys were caught up in the general restlessness of the post-Revolutionary period and by the autumn of 1789 were thinking of moving to the frontier. Young Levi, who was four years old at the time, remembered the trek west the following spring, made by the family group consisting of his grandfather and father (both Obadiahs), his two uncles, his two-year-old sister, and Sukey, a girl brought up by his grandfather. His brother, Samuel, who had been born in February, was ill and stayed behind in his mother's care. He does not mention any older women in the party, although later his grandmother and aunts were in the family circle. His mother and brother came west a few months later.

The Beardsleys bought their land from Goldsboro Banyer, one of the colonial and post-Revolutionary land speculators, near the northern border of Otsego County, just north of Cooper's holdings, west and a little south of Richfield Springs (a state historic marker identifies the place) but they did not go to that site at first. Rather the family rented the old Herkimer farm (also identifiable by a marker) at the foot of Canadarago Lake now on Route 28. This had been cleared and operated before the Revolution and apparently was in good enough shape to plant that spring of 1790.

Getting there was something more of a problem. They had difficulties, as did so many other pioneers, getting their livestock across the Hudson at Waterford. Then they followed the old road along the north bank of the Mohawk to Fonda where they crossed and continued west to Canajoharie. From there they took advantage of the roads cut by Clinton's soldiers over the hills to Springfield. Contemporary motorists will be pleased to discover that Seeber's Lane, which Beardsley mentions, still leads out of Canajoharie and is still so named.

Beardsley notes the lack of breadstuffs that spring of 1790, due to the bad crops the fall before. William Cooper tells of that famine and how he brought into his own settlements loads of provisions. He recalls that many were driven to drinking maple syrup and eating the wild leeks. "The quantity of leeks they eat had such an effect upon their breath that they could be smelled at many paces distant, and when they came together, it was like cattle that had been pastured in a garlic field."

While Beardsley speaks of his family as being poor, their livestock, horses, sheep, and hogs present a far more prosperous entourage than the lone pioneer with his wife, axe, pack, and gun he mentions as commonplace in another passage. A family group of men, such as the Beardsleys, were at a distinct advantage—for there were never enough hands in the early settlements. Being able to rent the Herkimer place gave them many other advantages. They got their crops in without having to clear land first and so insured their first winter's food for family and beasts; in the meantime they made a path to their own acres, six miles away, cleared a little land, and built their cabins. All this was far more carefully planned and executed than was typical. It also reflects the shrewd foresight and ripe wisdom that later characterized Levi and his brother in their legal careers.

Beardsley is not so good at sketching character as Wright, and members of his family do not come into sharp focus. One guesses something about his grandfather from his blithe assumption that he could tan a skin as well as any Indian, but his father and mother never emerge as more than shadows. The scene in which his mother spends her first night in a doorless cabin, terrified by the piercing cries of the forest, haunted by memories of Indians during the Revolution, is a classic vignette which in one form or another reappears frequently in the annals of the frontier. This, however, was not the kind of situation that sent the women whimpering to their corners; the real danger lay in the unrelieved loneliness of the isolated settlements, the lack of normal communal relationships. Both of our writers describe the women's afternoon get-togethers and bees of various types; these were essential therapy and safety valves. Wolves and bears a woman could face, and the great trees and night cries were nothing compared to the total lack of human contacts beyond a husband and the children she bore him. If the social bees of women were a psychological necessity, so too were the wrestling matches of the men. The aggressions of their descendants are taken out on the golf ball, but these men had a direct and eminently satisfactory release in physical combat which, for the most part, lacked malice and venom.

The minuteness with which Beardsley details everyday features of frontier life is part of his great usefulness. He is, for example, most explicit about the steps by which a cabin was built, the way a dance was organized, where they had to go to get their grain milled. His emphasis on mills, of course, reminds us of how essential an institution the mill was; it did little good to grow wheat or corn or buckwheat if one had no way to have it made into flour. Grinding by hand with mortar and pestle was impossibly time-consuming. There was so much to do and so few hands to do it. A mill was essential—and when, as he reports, Tunnicliff built a lumber mill in the community, the whole process of settling was greatly speeded up; it then became possible to turn tree trunks into house beams and clapboards in a matter of minutes, whereas those processes had previously taken hours of work with axe and adze. Frame houses and barns quickly replaced the far less satisfactory log cabins.

Beardsley seldom waxes poetic except when he writes of the forest and streams. The memory of the woods in different seasons and in differing weather is sharp and clear. His descriptions of clearing the land and the forest fires to complete that process are among his most valuable passages, for he supplements both William Cooper's account in *A Guide in the Wilderness* and James Fenimore Cooper's account in *The Pioneers*. He is equally good at describing such occasions as the bear hunts or that fascinating passage when his father and uncles fought under the witness tree so that the memory of their property lines would stay green—an American version of the old English custom of beating the bounds, thrashing the adolescent boys at key points in the property boundaries of a rural area. I have never run across any other reference to this custom in our part of the world.

Since the theme of this little volume is boyhood and growing up, the passages from the *Reminiscences* close with Levi's going to practice law, but this represents only about a fifth of the whole volume. His adventures in Ohio, his forays at the bar and in politics, his acquaintance with many of the principal political figures of his day are left for another, later editor. His is an anecdotal volume, stressing his friendships, the gossip he heard, hunting, lawsuits, political maneuvers, business deals, and the very male world in which he was a convivial participant. It makes, one might add, good reading and especially good reading for one interested in the little facts of life that many nineteenth-century writers neglected. He became a distinguished lawyer and politician in the Democratic party, and ultimately President of the New York Senate. The book came out when he was sixty-seven (1852); one notes that the title page speaks of it as being "printed" rather than "published" and his introduction leads one to think it may have been originally intended for his personal distribution rather than general sale.

The Wrights, like the Beardsleys, had deep roots in Connecticut; Henry Clarke Wright (1797–1870) was born there in the town of Sharon. His father and mother had a total of eleven children, of whom he was the tenth. Like many Americans of his time his father, Seth Wright (1755–1829), had two occupations; he was a farmer, but he was also a housebuilder or "house-joiner." By the time they moved to Otsego County his oldest son was twenty-two and mature enough to run the farm so that Seth was free to build houses and barns for the ever-flowing tide of newcomers.

Henry remembered leaving Sharon when he was in his fourth year, although his father may have leased his 142 acres (Wright remembered it as 160 acres) in Otsego County as early as 1797, the year Henry was born. The journey west was as memorable for him as was Levi Beardsley's—especially the crossing of the Hudson, where the Wrights came close to tragedy. The farm Seth Wright acquired was about four miles south of Hartwick, just off Route 205. The presence of a sawmill above the farm must have been one of its great advantages to a house-joiner.

Otego Creek (which Wright erroneously calls Otsego Creek) creates one of those delightful little valleys which are so characteristic of upstate New York. The farm lay along the eastern hillside; the little stream he describes still flows through the property into Otego Creek. The swamp which seemed a brooding presence is still to be seen but would no longer scare even the most timid child. Even today the area is unspoiled and the forests are in view; pastures that nourished the family cows nourish other cows in our time.

In an introductory section to *Human Life* which I have omitted, Wright makes an interesting sociological observation about frontier family life, namely that it was the responsibility of husbands and sons to supply the raw materials of food and raiment for the family; it was the duty of women to prepare these for use. Thus it was that the seven sons all learned farming and the four daughters cooking, spinning, weaving, and knitting. But the boys also learned other crafts besides, so that each had two strings to his bow. Some of them were apprenticed as dyers and cloth dressers; three were housebuilders like their father; and Henry, as we shall see, was apprenticed to a hatmaker.

Compared to Beardsley, Wright is immeasurably more complex; Beardsley's mind reminds one of hand-woven linen, all of a piece, each thread clearly to be seen, while Wright recalls a tartan of dark greens and blues with contrasting threads of yellow, pink, and red. The pacifist Wright is forever at war with the puritan tradition and the Congregational Church in which he was raised, and he suffered more than most men from the ambivalence he felt toward his father.

As a grown man Henry Wright remembered the two quite different facets of his father's personality. For the outsiders Seth Wright was a big, well developed, agile man, free and joyous, of a happy turn of mind, but this was not the side he saved for his family. At home he was stern, demanding immediate obedience, controlling his family with a tap of his foot or a look. Remembering that Henry Wright became a devout pacifist, it is probably significant that his earliest memory of his father was leading a military band dressed in his regimentals, his cocked hat, his epaulettes, and in his hand a drawn sword. The piece they were playing was "Heavenly Union."

If the Calvinist, warrior, and disciplinarian in his father offended Wright, he was never able to escape his affection and admiration for a man whose integrity, as he said, was not spoiled by his religion. He tells and comments upon an incident from his earliest years which is significant of both father and son: "There was a great scarcity of corn. The crops had been cut short generally. My father had had a large crop of Indian corn the previous year, and when there was none to be had elsewhere, he had a good supply. One morning, a man came from a distance to get a bushel of Indian corn. My father went to his corn barn to let him have it. I went with him. He measured it out, and put it into his bag. The man took out three dollars, and handed it to him in payment for the corn—that being the current price per bushel. My father took the money, changed it, and handed back one dollar and three quarters, retaining only one dollar and a quarter. The man was surprised, and asked him why he did not take the three dollars, as that was the common price. My father replied, that one dollar and a quarter would give him a just remuneration, and he could not thrive by taking advantage of the misfortunes of others to enrich himself. The beauty of this act I understood and appreciated; his religious observances I did not comprehend. I saw not their use; I saw not how they benefitted God or man."

Religion pervaded the Wright home. The family was raised on the Westminster Catechism, they were regular at church meetings, all the children were baptized. Every morning saw the Bible being read, there were prayers morning and evening, grace at the table, and careful observance of the Sabbath, fast, and thanksgiving days. Most of all there was overwhelming veneration for The Book, kept on its special shelf by the fireplace, read in a sanctified voice, referred to as the arbiter of life's every crucial decision. Against all this in due time Henry Wright was to revolt, but he was always a profoundly religious man, emphasizing over and over again that only by actions of love and kindness was salvation to be achieved. Let him state his own case:

"I believe in the existence of a God of justice and love; who made man, and put him under laws which are holy, just and good, and which cannot be violated with impunity. Though He exists separate from and independent of man and this universe, yet he can be truly loved and worshipped by us only in the exercise of affection, and of just and kindly offices towards our fellow-men. To love them with a love that seeketh not her own, is to love God; and to hate them, is to hate God; to do good to men, and to prepare ourselves for this work, is our only true and acceptable worship of the Deity. What is called God by Christendom and Heathendom, is but a convenient cover for the crimes that men perpetrate on men, under the names of war and slavery. . . . I would love and serve my Maker by loving and serving my fellow-beings; and dwell in Him by dwelling in his children. I would worship Him whom I have not seen, by exercising love and good-will towards those whom I have seen. A religion and a God that sanctify slavery, and war, and every crime, in this world, can do nothing for us in any other state of existence."

Wright's rejection of the Jehovah, God of Wrath, of his ancestors, propelled him into the midst of every reform movement of the mid-nineteenth century. He was an abolitionist, of course, but more compellingly he was a pacifist and he hated every manifestation of rule by force. He had very advanced ideas about education, about women's rights and about children's rights, he was a teetotaler, he disapproved of smoking, rich foods, and fancy clothes. He disapproved of lawyers and courts almost as much as he did churches. In some ways he was also a good deal of a bore, as reformers are apt to be.

The death of his mother, his father's remarriage, and the death of his brother all shortly after arrival in Otsego County were unquestionably shocks for young Henry but these were all in the pattern of Nature's laws. What gives one pause is the role he played in his father's house. His stepmother had a house full of grown boys and new babies of her own and as he grew older Henry found himself baby-sitting and, more than that, doing many of the chores that older daughters in the house would have been doing had there been any. This raises interesting questions. He cleaned, he cooked, he washed; he didn't spin or weave, but he wound the thread on spools ready for the weaver, he actively partook of the feminine roles in frontier life. When he writes of this he writes defensively and one says, "Dear friend, thou dost protest too much." Wright makes it abundantly clear that he also fulfilled the male roles on the farm, milking, riding the horses, yoking and driving the oxen, bringing in the cows, harvesting, and all the rest of the hard labor of the frontier farmer. But Wright lived in a world where there was little question about what roles people played in life—a man had his work cut out for him and it didn't include baby-sitting and dishwashing. One wonders, despite his vehement disclaimer of ever having been taunted for these activities, if his later rejection of many of the normal male activities may not have stemmed from a duality he acted out at home. He deplored fishing, hunting, the militia, rough sports, all the recreations of the man-world, and in their place he substituted his neo-puritanism and reformism. While sympathetic with many of his objectives, I find myself wondering about the psychological patterns of this over-gentle, over-vehement, introverted child-man.

Two of the most interesting sections in Wright's memoirs are those of Aunt Huldah and his adventures in school. The scenes in which Old Auntie, children gathered about her, told of witches, ghosts, and Indian tortures are a contribution of the first order to American folklore, for here we see the folk narrative in the process of transmission and there is sufficient emphasis on the setting so that we see why it had the impact it did. His educational experiences are equally fascinating: the black snake that went to school, the terrifying drunken master, the wise and gentle schoolmistress are valuable contributions to case histories of education on the frontier. In a world where older boys could seldom be spared from farm work, except in the winter, education had its special problems— especially as those boys, often young men, actually, had only a minimum of interest in learning anything. The violences reported in the schools of the great cities of our own time had their counterpart in many a one-room school on the frontier.

His accounts of his apprenticeship and his conversion are two major contributions to our knowledge of frontier life which also deserve notice. His description of his apprenticeship as a hatmaker, at a time when the apprentice system was in decay, is significant. The jolt of being lifted out of a devout, Bible-encircled home and thrown among a lot of hard-drinking, profane, and ribald journeymen led to Wright's first awareness that the Calvinist world he had known was surrounded by another world, totally pagan. The realization came at a time when he was suffering from acute homesickness, which must have intensified what would in any event have been a shocking experience.

Wright is both likable and irritating. His picture of himself as the oldest apprentice, sharing all his goodies but refusing to accept anything from his young friends, is the picture of an insufferable prig. Fortunately we see many more attractive aspects of him.

He often agonizes over his experiences with the naivete of an adolescent. This quality is useful when he writes about his religious conversion, for one recaptures something of the momentousness of the step. The earlier passages in which he describes church services, his attitude toward the clergy, his doubts and haunting fears add intensity to his final step of acceptance of the ways of his forefathers. His later revolt against those ways is beyond the scope of this volume. Yet, how seldom we read so personal an account of what the great revivals meant to the individuals who were emotionally caught up in those high dramas of frontier religion.

Wright never worked as a hatter; he left his apprenticeship uncompleted by mutual agreement with David Bright, "the Boss." He went to Andover to study for the ministry and in due time he was licensed to preach, holding a parish for eight years in Newbury, New Hampshire. The marriage he entered into at twenty-six seems not to have flourished and he was much too unconventional for his ecclesiastical peers. His long devotion to reform movements began with his rejection of alcohol, but the pattern of his life was set when he met William Lloyd Garrison in 1835.

John L. Thomas in *The Liberator: William Lloyd Garrison; A Biography* (1963) calls Wright "the most durable of Garrisonian radicals" and quotes Garrison's description of him as "a most valuable acquisition to our cause—a fearless, uncompromising and zealous Christian." As

Thomas points out, Garrison could have added that he was also restless, vain, and querulous. Wright became an agent for the American Sunday School Union, Children's Agent for New England. He was the author of two books on marital relations: *Marriage and Parentage* and *The Unwelcome Child* (1858). He was also greatly attracted to the non-resistance movement. While he was ardent in all these causes, he would drop any of them for the cause of peace, and one is not at all surprised to know that he was a member of William Ladd's Peace Society. His admiration and friendship for Garrison lasted all his life; despite the many broken friendships both of them suffered, this relationship held firm until Wright's death.

In their later years, like many of the best minds of their time, both Garrison and Wright were sincere believers in spiritualism. Wright died in Pawtucket, Rhode Island, in the summer of 1870; Garrison delivered a notable funeral sermon but shortly thereafter was taken very ill and could not see to purchasing a burial plot for his old friend who had temporarily been placed in a crypt. In September Garrison went to a "healing medium" in Boston for medical advice. After this had been given, the medium reported that Henry was waiting to talk to him. The message was explicit: bury him in the single triangular plot, under a tree in the northwest portion of the cemetery where his body was stored. Greatly relieved, Garrison went to Pawtucket to find the plot, but the assistant superintendent of the cemetery couldn't find a triangular single plot with a tree. It wasn't until a second visit and with the help of the superintendent himself that they found a little forgotten lot, just the right size and just as Henry had described it to Garrison from the other side.

The purpose of this book is limited to portraying boyhood on the frontier, but students of the reform movements in this country and of nineteenth-century religious history would do well to turn to *Human Life* and read it *in toto.* I can discover little about the history of the book; it is seldom referred to and only a few of the major libraries seem to own copies. It is a neglected nugget of American social history and the mirror of a lovable and infuriating man.

Calvinism and his ultimate revolt against it colored both Wright's boyhood and manhood. Beardsley's people were Episcopalians and while he says little or nothing about it, one assumes that religion played a minor but satisfactory role in his life. On the other hand, Beardsley pays considerable attention to politics, militia, and the law, matters that Wright ignored except to excoriate lawyers, judges, and the military.

There are interesting areas where both writers agree. For both, the forest with its infinite stillness and majesty was almost a religious experience. Their accounts of farm chores, maple sugaring, bees, and other aspects of social life are similar but always colored by their adult views. Their views of themselves as boys are almost identical: Wright says, "I had unbounded confidence in myself, and laughed at difficulties. My spirit was buoyant, confident, restless and impatient under restraints not self-imposed." In similar vein, Beardsley, recounting his successes in the little school to which he went, says that he "never doubted but what I could do anything that others could. This impression has been a leading one through life, and to my perseverance in it, I have ascribed much of my success." Out of their self-confidence came very different careers, but each gained a measure of success and fame— Beardsley by fitting into the establishment with ease and harmony, Wright by speaking out for that little minority that was at odds with all the common assumptions of his time.

Wright has great heart, gentleness, and courage but not

one iota of humor. Beardsley, on the other hand, is best
described in the words he applied to a friend of his when
he said of him that he "took the world easy, laughed at its
follies, submitted to its crosses and murmured not at its
reverses." They represent constant types in American life,
they seldom care much for each other but the country
always will need both the worldly man of law and order
and it will need equally the rebel, bitten by divine dis-
content.

A word or two about the texts. So far as I am aware,
neither of these books went beyond a single edition; at
any rate these are the only editions I have seen: *Human
Life Illustrated in My Individual Experience as a Child, A
Youth, and a Man* by Henry Clarke Wright, Boston, pub-
lished by Bela Marsh, 25 Cornwall, 1849; *Reminiscences;
Personal and other incidents, early settlement of Otsego
County; notices and anecdotes of Public Men; Judicial
and Legal and Legislative Matters; Field Sports Disser-
tations*. By Levi Beardsley, Esq., late of the New-York
Senate, and President thereof. New-York: Printed by
Charles Vinten, 100 Nassau Street, 1852.

In general I have left spelling and punctuation as in the
originals except when changes in usage have altered or
clouded the meaning. I have regularized the paragraph-
ing, especially in Beardsley, to aid a generation hellbent
for rapid reading. I have curbed Beardsley's passion for
the italic, substituting modern punctuation.

The Beardsley text is almost completely intact. I have,
however, cut many long passages from Wright because
his constant sermonizing went beyond the purpose of this
book. I have tried to leave just enough of these passages
to give a strong sense of the author's introverted and complex personality.

Finally, thanks to four old friends: my colleague, Dor-
othy C. Barck, Librarian Emeritus of the New York State

Historical Association, whose encyclopedic knowledge of New York bibliography has aided me as it has hundreds of better scholars before me; Roy L. Butterfield, Otsego County Historian and model for all local historians, who first called *Human Life* to my attention and who helpfully read the manuscript; Mrs. Marjorie Willsey, long my assistant, who typed the manuscript and caught not a few of the *gaffes*; my wife, Agnes Halsey Jones, whose ever-inquiring mind and wise encouragement are responsible for most of what I accomplish.

LOUIS C. JONES

New York State Historical Association
Cooperstown, New York
Spring, 1964

BIBLIOGRAPHY

Beardsley, Levi. *Reminiscences.* New York: Privately printed, 1852.

Butterfield, Roy L. *In Old Otsego.* Cooperstown: Otsego Co. Board of Supervisors, 1959.

Cooper, James Fenimore. *The Pioneers.* 2 vols. New York: Charles Wiley, 1823.

Cooper, William. *A Guide in the Wilderness.* Dublin: Gilbert & Hodges, 1810; Reprint. Rochester: George P. Humphrey, 1897.

Garrison, Wendell Phillips and Garrison, Francis Jackson. *William Lloyd Garrison 1805–1879.* 4 vols. New York: The Century Co., 1889.

Hurd, D. Hamilton. *History of Otsego County.* Philadelphia: Everts & Fariss, 1878.

Thomas, John L. *The Liberator: William Lloyd Garrison; A Biography.* Boston: Little, Brown, 1963.

Wright, Henry Clarke. "Diary, October 22, 1852–March 15, 1853." Unpublished manuscript owned by the New York State Historical Association, Cooperstown, New York.

————. *Human Life.* Boston: Bela Marsh, 1849.

————. *The Unwelcome Child.* Boston: Bela Marsh, 1858.

FROM

Levi Beardsley's

Reminiscences

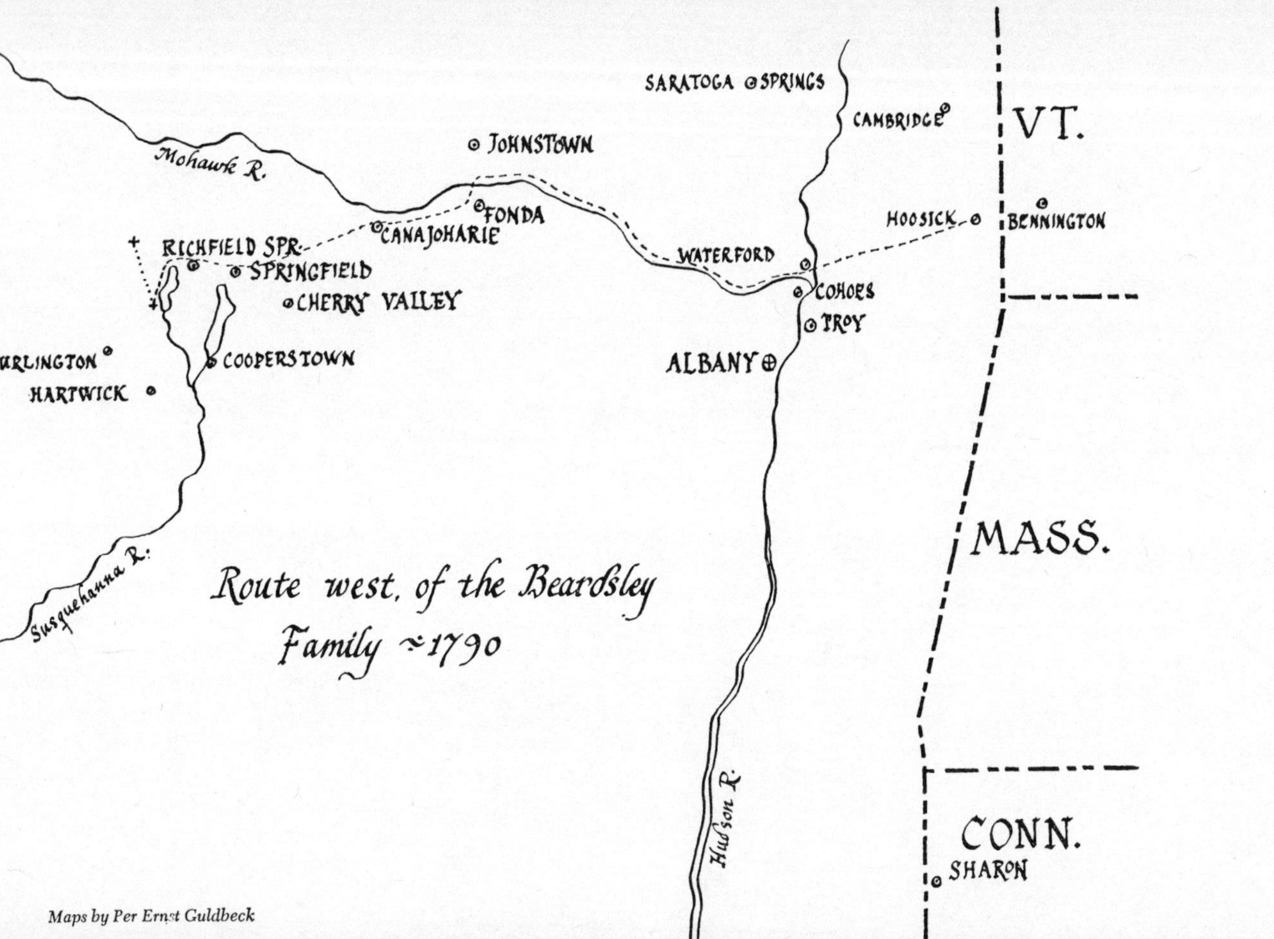

Maps by Per Ernst Guldbeck

I

I HAVE a distinct recollection of some events as far back as the summer of 1789; when I was in my fourth year. I remember going to a funeral in Bennington, at the burial of a man named Porter, who died suddenly. It was summer, for the red cherries were then ripe. This might have been the summer of 1788, but I think it could not have been so far back, though I recollect something, that took place in November or December of that year or the winter of '89; as I went with my parents to a country store, where I first saw a stove and a negro. The stove I recollect, from putting my hand on it and getting burned, and the negro, from being afraid of him.

In the latter part of '89 or early part of '90, there was a remarkable exhibition of northern lights, which formed a beautiful crown over head, bright and nearly red, which my childish imagination turned into cart wheels, from its forming many circles resembling wheels. It was so brilliant, that my father went out and read by its light. This exhibition was afterwards remembered and talked about, and as the French revolution soon after broke out, which was ultimately attended with horrible cruelties, some who had seen this aurora borealis, superstitiously regarded it as the precursor of that bloody revolution.

In the autumn of '89 my father, with his brothers and

my grandfather, made up their minds to emigrate to the west the next spring, and settle in the woods, on new land which they had selected and purchased of Goldsbro Banyer, of Albany, at $1.25 per acre. The land was in what is now Richfield, Otsego county. The spring of 1790 having sold their farm in Hoosic, my father, with two of his brothers, who had small families, and my grandfather, broke up and started for their intended new home.

Their worldly substance was small. I think for the purpose of moving, they had a cart and one or two wagons, one or two yoke of oxen, three or four horses, and a few cattle, sheep and hogs. The roads were excessively bad, and they took but little household stuff with them; nor could they, as their means of transportation were very limited. I was little more than four years old; being four in November preceding, and this movement commenced the latter part of April, 1790. My mother was left behind with a sick child, who had been dangerously ill, and was not well enough to be removed. My sister, about two years younger than myself, was with me, stowed away in the cart or wagon, among the chairs and furniture, and put under the care of a girl brought up by my grandfather.

I recollect a few incidents of the journey. We crossed the Hudson near Half Moon (Waterford) where a young bull jumped out of the ferry boat, and swam back to the eastern shore. He was finally driven up and made to swim to the western side, to join the other cattle. We then passed to the Mohawk, and kept up that river on the north side, till we came to Fonda's ferry, which must have been very near the present village of Fonda. Here we ferried over to the south side and continued up the river to Canajoharie.

I well remember the appearance of the elm trees that skirted the Mohawk, with their large swelling buds and spring-like appearance. At Canajoharie we left the river and took the old continental road, as it was called, towards Springfield, Otsego County; the same road that a division of the American army had taken to Otsego lake under Gen. Clinton, to join Sullivan's expedition against the Indians.

We staid all night at Conradt Seeber's (now Seeber's lane,) where he kept a poor Dutch tavern. Slavery was then common, and not regarded a sin as now. Every Dutch farmer who was able to purchase, had more or less slaves; and negroes generally fared as well as their masters. I was somewhat afraid of the "darkies" but became more reconciled to them when they spoke kindly to me, in broken English. Bread stuffs, were very scarce and dear that year, all over the country, and in Europe too. We had got out of bread and flour and could get nothing of the kind at Seeber's, or among his neighbours. The negroes were sent out, from house to house, but could get nothing in the bread line but *potatoes*, which we roasted, and I went to sleep, after eating some of them, crying for bread.

The next day we started and went as far as William Seeber's, with the teams, about three miles; where they concluded to leave part of the vehicles till the roads became settled, which were then broken up and almost impassable. Some of the party drove the live stock, and went on the best way they could. My father put a saddle on one of the horses, and on another packed a bed and bedding on which the girl was to ride. I was placed on the horse behind him on a pillow tied to the saddle, with a strap under my arms, buckled around his waist, to prevent me from falling off, and carrying my sister before him, we pursued our journey; the girl (Sukey) riding the other horse on top of the bed and bedding; and a yearling colt tagging after. This constituted the cavalcade so far as my father and his family were concerned.

Our object was to go up towards Springfield till we

reached the old road, that diverged and ran off west or southwesterly, to the foot of Schuyler's lake, where my father and uncles had hired the "Herkimer farm" on which was a small improvement made before the war; and two small log houses, more properly speaking huts. We went about half way that day and stopped overnight in a log house, about two miles west of Little Lakes, and a mile east of what is now Richfield Springs, from which stopping place we continued next day down the lake, on the east side to its foot.

In due time after the roads were settled, the teams were sent back for the cart, wagons and furniture, and after planting a small piece of corn, my father took one of the horses and went to Hoosic for my mother. She rode the horse on a man's saddle, and carried the child, my father in patriarchal manner walking by her side; and thus the family were at length re-united in the woods at the foot of the beautiful lake, and by the side of the fine little stream known as "Herkimer Creek," then full of fish, particularly the speckled trout.

After his return, one of the first things for the safety of the sheep, was to build a fold or place where they could be kept at night, safe from the depredations of wolves, whose nocturnal howlings on the hills, east of the lake could be heard almost every night during that season. A pen was formed by laying up logs like the body of a log house, and so close and high that a wolf could not get in, or over it. In this the sheep were driven every night. I recollect the putting up of this pen. Timothy Morse, who had recently settled at Burlington, was there to assist, and being a very strong man carried up one of the corners. He was afterwards Justice of the Peace, and a Judge of the Court of Common Pleas, when I was admitted to the bar.

After the weeding of the corn, and before and after the hay making season, my father and his two brothers went to work, and cut and cleared out a path through the woods from the foot of the lake to their lot in Richfield. They followed the marked trees on the line of lots as near as the ground would admit, and made a road or path, wide enough for a cart to get along with skilful driving, about six miles, or as the road ran a little more. The path being prepared, they went to work whenever they could be spared from the farm at the lake, and cut away the brush and small trees, and enough of the large ones to afford room for building two log houses, one on my father's farm the other on my uncle's, the houses being twenty or twenty-five rods apart. These were put up and partly completed in the course of the summer, that they might move to them in August or September, after securing the small crops. They were placed in the woods, and not an eighth of an acre cleared around either, or even both of them, and were anything but habitable.

The one we moved in, for my father moved to his one or two days before my uncle, was a small log cabin, the body laid up, and part, though not the whole of the roof was covered with black ash and elm bark, which had been peeled from the trees at the season when bark is taken off easily. When spread out and put on the roof and pressed down with poles or small timbers, the rough side, exposed to the weather, it makes a good roof that will last several years, and shed the rain quite well. Our house was partially covered, and when it rained we had to put our effects and get ourselves under that part which was sheltered. The floor was made of bass wood logs, split and hewed partially on one side, and then spotted down, making a good substantial floor, but only about half of ours was laid. We had no fire place or chimney, and till this was built, the cooking must all be done out of doors. A place for the door was cut out, so that we could go in, but no door had been made, nor had we any means of fastening the doorway except by barricading. There was of course no chamber floor, though this was supplied by loose boards, subsequently obtained.

A mud and stick chimney and fire place were afterwards added, as the weather became cool; and to get earth or clay to make mortar to daub the house and make the chimney, a hole was dug under the floor, which was our only cellar, in which in winter we put a few bushels of potatoes and turnips, and took up one of the flattened logs from the floor whenever we wanted any thing from below.

I have said there was no door when we moved in. My father on reaching the house with my mother and family, remained there the first night, hanging a blanket at the door way to keep out part of the night air. The next day he returned to the lake, with the team to assist my uncle to move up with his family, two days after we came. Thus my mother and myself with the two younger children were left in the woods alone for a day and a night, five or six miles from our recent residence, and without any fastening to the doorway in case we wanted to close the entrance. It must be recollected that this was but a few years after the close of the war, and all the recollections of Indian atrocities were fresh in remembrance among those who had gone through the revolutionary scenes. My mother, with probably as much courage as most women, and with more fortitude than many of them, was timid in regard to Indians. She and her sisters had narrowly escaped those that passed through Cambridge [New York] on their way to Bennington. Her cousin, John Younglove, an ardent whig, had been shot in his own house by Indians, or Tories disguised in Indian dresses.

During the day, after my father had gone with the team, we heard noises in the woods, screaming, and to us very frightful. I suppose it must have been blue jays, with the hootings of the owl; but we converted them into the possible, if not probable noise of lurking Indians. What was to be done? We had no door to the house, but mother went to work, to barricade and secure the doorway; which she soon rendered quite safe by bedsteads, chairs, tables, and other household furniture. The gun had been left at home, well loaded, and she said if we were attacked, she would defend the house, though she knew but little about the use of fire arms, except to load. She examined the powder horn, to see how much powder we had, and the bullet pouch to see how many balls; and being thus prepared, secured and fortified, we passed that night safely, annoyed more by mosquitos than anything else; and the next day, father with my uncle and family returned.

He brought with him some pieces of boards to make a door, which he soon completed, with wooden hinges and wooden catch and latch, raised by a string; and the door was fastened by a pin inside, when we wanted to secure it. "The latch string however of that cabin was always out," except when the family were from home; and here we were settled on our new farm, in the midst of the woods, five miles from our neighbours, except my uncle and his family.

Let me go back for a few moments to our residence at the lake before we removed to the farm. I want to let my readers into the secrets of living in a new country, the privations and hardships, incident to such a life. You will probably, many of you, never know them from experience, but I will give you an insight.

We all came to the country quite poor. There were no stores near us, and if there had been we had nothing to pay for goods. Our nearest mill while we lived at the lake was Tubb's, on Oak's Creek, near Toddsville, some three miles from Cooperstown. After we went to Richfield, we sometimes went to this mill, sometimes to Walbridges, in

Burlington, and sometimes to Fort Plain; the latter at least thirty miles, as the road then ran. In the year 1791, Wm. Tunnicliff built a saw mill, near Richfield springs, four miles from our residence; and the next year he built on the opposite side of the creek a small grist mill, which served the purposes of the townspeople for several years, except in low water when they had to go greater distances. Judge Peck was the millwright and built both mills; the mill dam, put in by him in 1791, is still standing; and the old building in which was the grist mill, though removed, is also standing, used for a shed; the shingle roof put on at the time, being quite perfect yet.

Almost every family in the country made their own cloth. The dye tub was always an appendage, and stood in the corner near the fire, and served as a seat for one of the inmates. We came to the country before sheep shearing, so we had to wait till they were sheared and the wool picked, carded, spun, wove and dressed, before we had our annual supply of woollen clothing; and for linen we had to wait till we could raise flax and manufacture it. To obviate the difficulty, so far as I was concerned, my mother, after she came to the lake, cut up an old cloak, and from it made me a little coat with pockets.

My grandfather professed a knowledge in the tanning business, and having provided himself with a large trough in which he put such skins as he could get; he put them through his process of tanning. I don't think he knew much about it except in reference to deer skins; he could dress them in Indian fashion (smoke dressed) as well as any Mohawk or Iroquois. He however got a sheep skin and having taken off the wool, went on to dress it. I think the dressing was but little more than rubbing and pulling it and then nailing it to the wagon box to dry, after stretching it every way to its utmost tension. He declared it fit for use, and it was decided, in council, that for want of something better, I should have a pair of sheepskin breeches, which were soon prepared, and I was cased in them. The skin was dry and rattled like parchment or an old snuff bladder, and the garment was so short in the legs that they extended but about half way below my knees. You may judge of my appearance; the old sheepskin when dry, would rattle when I ran, and if the pants got wet they would stretch and become flabby, and then harder and shorter than ever when they got dry again.

Thus pantalooned and coated, I spent a very pleasant summer and for amusement often went out with David, my father's youngest brother, some 14 years of age. The marshy land abounded with English snipe, which you know sit so close to the ground, and so resemble it in color that you can hardly see them, till they get on wing. Just at night they delight in getting up, and with a spiral whirl, ascend high into the air, with a constant gyration, chirping, as they rise till they are out of sight, and almost of hearing; and then will come down again, and settle very near where they started from, crying as they squat on the ground "quaack."

Uncle David used to arm himself with a long brushy stick, with his pocket full of stones, and on seeing the bird get up would place himself near where he started from, and when he settled down would frequently kill him with his brushy stick. Sometimes he would kill him with stones, and to promote this desirable object, my coat pockets were filled with "rocks," as the Buck Eyes say, for him to heave at them. The cloth being old and tender, from which my coat was made, the pockets were soon torn out, and I was threatened with a severe chastisement for thus destroying my new coat.

The farm at the lake was retained a second year, my grandfather and one of my uncles residing there during the year 1791, and was kept for the common benefit of the colony, to furnish hay and grain, till we could clear the land and raise crops in Richfield.

It is time to go back again to our log house on the new farm. In the course of the autumn of 1790, and during '91, many people came to look for lands, and my father's and uncle's houses, were places of rendezvous for all comers. They generally slept on the floor before the fire on straw beds; for we had scarcely a spare one of other description at that time. After a chamber floor was put in, some slept in the chamber, to which they ascended by a ladder that always stood in the house.

II

I shall never forget the freshness and beauty of the forest, after winter had passed away. The spring flowers were everywhere in bloom, the herbage high and luxuriant covered the ground, the wild leek was green and so abundant that it was used as a substitute for onions; the nettles were frequently four feet high, and the ground yew, or running hemlock, with its woody vine, often ten feet long and standing two or three feet above the surface, spread over many acres, presenting a formidable obstruction to the pedestrian, particularly if he was barefooted, as men and boys generally went in the summer season.

The winter had passed off, and during the whole of it, the cattle had been sustained by occasionally a little hay and straw and a few ears of corn; relying principally on browsing, which is feeding on the tops of trees that were daily felled for them. They lived through the winter quite well, and soon became thrifty [*i.e.*, flourishing] and sleek after the herbage had sprung up. This browsing was resorted to frequently, and almost every year more or less up to 1801–2.

Those only who have resided in a new country, where forest scenery in all its richness and beauty is presented to the view, can realize how strongly those recollections are impressed on the mind. It is no marvel to me, that the red man sighs for forest life, where, without restraints, imposed by laws and customs of civilized society, he roams free as the air he breathes. To the man of reflection, who feels responsible to a higher power, and looks upon the objects around him as evidence of the existence of that great and good being, who created, regulates, and sustains all things, I can conceive of no place or circumstance so well calculated to impress the sensitive mind with awe and veneration, as the deep seclusion of the forest. Often, very often, when a mere boy, have I repaired to a secluded spot, where there was a clump of pine trees, and sat under them for hours together, listening to the sighing of the winds in the topmost branches. The slightest motion of air might be heard, in fact, I have hardly ever known the atmosphere so still, that it did not agitate and rustle through the tops of those evergreens. If it was but a slight breeze it produced a soothing hum, well calculated to calm the mind and induce contemplation; while if the blast was violent, there was the loud resounding roar through the branches; giving incontestible proof that the "stormy king" could invigorate those gentle gales and convert them to the more stern exhibitions of "storm and tempest." What temple "made with hands" so raises the feelings of the contemplative mind, as the vast creation of forest, river and lake? . . .

For several years each family made its own cloth, from wool and flax; and even sacks and coarse garments from nettles, which were strong and durable like hempen cloth. It must be borne in mind that carding and picking machines had not then been invented, and if they had, were not introduced in the country till many years afterwards. The sheep being washed and sheared, the wool must first be picked by hand, and this was generally done by the family in the evening; then it must be greased and broke as they called it, and afterwards carded into rolls by hand, when it was fit for spinning. Each family kept a great wheel, and a little wheel, the first for wool and tow, and the other for flax; many also had a loom, for almost every family wove their own cloth, either at home or at their neighbours. At my father's they had a loom and each kind of wheel, and after the country became settled and we had advanced a little—so as "to be able to do in the world," as the old women used to say—we always had a spinning girl, and sometimes two, a considerable part of each season.

Our mode of life for several years was plain, coarse and primitive. Tea was scarcely known, and not at all as a common beverage, till three or four years after we were settled. Coffee was not introduced till several years later. Sugar was made from the maple every spring, and salt obtained from Albany in small quantities. I think we had been in the country three or four years, before any one thought of buying tea, except perhaps a quarter or half pound of "bohea" [China black tea], which was only doled out, when the women came together for an afternoon visit, and then only to them; labouring men did not expect it.

A substitute for tea and coffee was often procured from a root that grew in wet ground, which was called "evin root," but I do not know its botanical name [nor could the editor discover it]. When boiled, the decoction was somewhat of a chocolate colour, though rather inclining to purple. The flavour was remarkably pleasant when sweetened, and was generally preferred to tea. The inner portion of white pine bark, when boiled, and sweetened, makes a pleasant drink, and so does the sassafras root.

Let me describe those early female visits. A lady wanted her neighbours to come and make her a visit and spend the afternoon; mind you, an afternoon; the meaning of which was, to come as soon as they had the dishes washed after dinner, which was at twelve o'clock. They would come on foot three miles, and remain as late as they could, and reach home in time to milk the cows at night. They always had their tea as early as five or six o'clock, and those farthest off then started for home, through the woods. Some were timid and afraid of bears, and with those, some one would go and see them safely through swamps, and dangerous places. Sometimes a bear would present himself, just to frighten them, but generally scampered off; for it is seldom that he will make an attack, unless very hungry, or when young ones are in peril.

Generally speaking, the ladies were resolute; and went everywhere without fear. Their dress was plain, cheap and simple. A black skirt, and white or calico short gown, with occasionally a full calico, or chintz dress, constituted the top of the fashion. High heeled shoes were worn, which were fastened and adorned by a small buckle. Sometimes a cap was worn, but not generally for the first few years. A bonnet constituted the head dress, which on being laid aside, the head was without covering. It was no uncommon thing, for several years, to see married, as well as young ladies, trudging along barefoot, with their shoes and stockings in their hands, to avoid getting them soiled with mud, and then putting them on before they entered the house.

It was quite common with the ladies, to couple with their visits a quilting, or spinning, or carding bee. The carding and quiltings were done at the house, where the visit or bee was to be consummated. The spinning was a different affair. When a spinning bee was to come off, the wool or flax in small quantities was distributed among the invited guests; and the day indicated when they were to bring in the yarn and drink tea. The yarn was returned, and the good dames drank their tea, talked over neighbourhood affairs, indulged in critical and sometimes even slanderous remarks, and then retired to their virtuous homes. To suppose there was no gossip and slander in the country, because it was new, would indicate but a superficial knowledge of female character.

I may as well throw together, in this place, the remarks intended to be made in reference to the early habits and modes of life, which will apply to a series of years after the settlement as well as the first few years; and as we had no aristocratic associations in those early times, my remarks apply to the bone and sinew, the real democracy of the country. Those men, with strong arms, hard hands, and iron frame, might daily be seen, wending their way with knapsack on their backs, an axe lashed on the outside, and with gun on their shoulder, seeking a favorite resting place, prepared to grapple with the hardships and privations of frontier life, till the forests could be prostrated, the country improved, and the modes of civilized life and luxurious living could take the place of unmitigated toil. Their wives, generally speaking, were equally industrious, and nobly sustained the exertions of their husbands.

The settlement of the town, after the first year or two, went on rapidly; men were rough and hardy, and all public occasions wound up with trials of strength. Wrestling, running, jumping, and hopping always constituted part of the amusements. Logging bees and raisings were of frequent occurrence. The party making the bee, or raising, furnished himself with some poor rum, as an indispensable article to ensure success; if he did not, he was regarded as a mean covetous fellow, and his work would be poorly done, if done at all. Whiskey was not then introduced, nor till several subsequent years.

After the building was raised, or the bee concluded, the party collected to take the last drink, and then the sports commenced. Almost invariably a ring was formed for wrestling, and frequently commenced with boys, the men looking on. The boy thrown would bring in one to wrestle with the victor, and so on till all had wrestled, and the one was victor, who could keep the ring against all comers; so also with the men, who never expected to separate without a goodly number of wrestling matches. This practice was very generally continued as late as 1807. I have never seen so good wrestlers as those early settlers in Richfield. . . .

I became skilful in all these sports, understood them well, and in a rough and tumble scuffle, or at side hold, there were but few of my age I could not throw. Every lock, in wrestling, was familiar, and I knew how and when to take them, and how and when to lay out my strength to accomplish my object. I was quick and but few men, even much larger and stronger than myself, but I could more than match.

I have spoken of logging. Having been familiar with clearing up new land from my early childhood, let me describe the process. The ground to be cleared being selected, the first move is to cut all the underbrush and small trees, generally called "staddles." The brush are trimmed out and heaped in suitable places, and all such small trees, as can conveniently be handled, are cut and thrown on the heaps, with the old fallen limbs of trees; the small ones being cut near the ground. You are now ready to cut the large timber; and here great judgment must be used in falling it, so that you can log it to advantage. Trees should be so fallen as to be parallel with each other, and if on hilly land, should be fallen in such a manner that on logging they may be rolled down hill. Those cut up should be in logs, fourteen or fifteen feet long, according to their size. By skilful falling much chopping may be saved, by leaving many large trees to be piled against, on making log heaps.

Hard timber, maple, beech, birch, and elm, predominated in that part of Otsego county; the timber being very heavy. A good chopper would cut his acre and pile the brush in seven or eight days; I have known it done in less. At the age of twenty-two years I could cut an acre in seven days, but as a general average men would be from seven to ten days, particularly if several worked together. Chopping is hard, but clean work, and I was fond of it. A man going into the woods with his axe soon makes an opening, which being enlarged daily, serves to encourage and stimulate him to vigorous action. The trees being chopped and brush piled, if done in May or June, should be left through July and August, by which time they become so dry that the fire frequently runs over the whole ground, burning all the brush, many of the logs, and blackening those that remain. This would be regarded as a "good burn," leaving the soil clean of weeds, and herbage. Then follows the logging and burning the log-heaps, most dirty, smoky, disagreeable work. Three men and a yoke of oxen would log an acre per day, sometimes more, if the timber was light, and well felled and cut. The ashes, worth 6¼ cents, must be scraped together, and carried to an ashery, to make black salts, and eventually pearl or potash. All this being done, the land was ready for harrowing and reception of seed; after which the fences could be made at pleasure.

It was not uncommon to make sugar in the spring, on a piece of forest land, and then clear it off for a crop of corn the same season. Several acres of my father's lands, where he afterwards planted his orchard, were thus used, and cleared off; the small brush had been cut the preceding autumn. When the time arrived for making sugar, the trees were tapped and a large quantity made. As the season advanced, we cut the small timber, heaped the brush, and got everything ready to cut the large trees, as soon as sugar making was over; that being past, we cut and burned all the timber, and cleared the land for a crop.

The month of May was warm and dry, when on burning the brush, the fire ran over all the ground clearing it of herbage, so that we had but little harrowing to do, to fit it for planting. It was nearly the first of June when we planted, but the corn was soon up, grew rapidly, and with but little more than one slight dressing with the hoe, we had fifty bushels of good corn to the acre, with any quantity of large yellow pumpkins. After the corn was planted, and the ground fenced, we had to trap and shoot the striped squirrels [chipmunks] to protect the corn, as those little animals have an inveterate desire to dig it up, to obtain the grain at the root.

Those burnings of new lands, in dry weather, frequently extend beyond the ground intended to be cleared, and rage furiously in the woods. Every one who has long resided in a new country has seen the woods on fire; nothing can be more grand than their appearance at night, when the fire rages among dry and partially decayed trees. The flames, as they are fanned by the breeze, seem to flash out and leap fitfully from tree to tree; then, subsiding for a moment, will break out again as the wind freshens. Frequently the fire rapidly ascends a dry tree till it reaches the topmost branches, and then becomes, from bottom to top, a mass of flame, vivid and transparent; the atmosphere becomes charged with smoke, the heavens enlightened by the thousand fires, the roar of the flames, the crackling of dry limbs and fagots, with the frequent thundering of the large trees as they fall to the ground, render the scene grand, imposing and magnificently brilliant. Cooper, in his *Pioneers*, has given a graphic picture of a burning forest, the best by far that I have seen; and yet grand and truthful as that description is, it comes far short of reality, as all know who have witnessed similar exhibitions.

It seems to me we had much more thunder during those early years than we have latterly; if it was so, it might have resulted from accidental and natural causes, some years more than others; or may there not be more electricity in the atmosphere, when a country is new and uncultivated, than after it is cleared and subjected to the free unobstructed rays of the sun?

I was caught out in a storm that made a very lively impression on my mind, as well as subjecting me to a tremendous drenching. I must have been thirteen or fourteen years of age, and had been sent that afternoon three miles to the nearest blacksmith to have the ploughshare sharpened. In those days we used the old-fashioned bull plough, with wrought iron coulters and shares, which frequently required sharpening. The share was put in one end of a bag, and the coulter in the other, and was thrown on the back of the old brown mare and I on the top of it.

In new countries, where there is not much work required from the blacksmith, except those occasional jobs, he generally works in the fields a large portion of time; and this was the case with the one whom I wanted to see. He came from the field, and though short of coal, managed to raise sufficient heat to do the work; but manifested no desire [to] hurry it. When he had got through, it was nearly night, and a thunder storm was coming from the west. He put the bag, with share and coulter on the mare, and I started for home. Nearly the whole way was through the woods, and my load being unequally balanced, I had to ride slow, so that before I was one-third of the way home, the storm was upon me. The rain poured down, the wind blew furiously, and the lightning was vivid and constant. It soon became so dark, that I could not see objects a yard from me, not even the horse's head, except by the glare of the lightning, when the flashes were so bright they seemed to blind me for a moment, and then left me in more than natural darkness. The only way for me, unless I abandoned the load, was to hold it on as well as possible, and let the mare take her own course but not go faster than a walk, as her trot would have thrown off the bag, and probably me with it.

The thunder followed the lightning in quick succession, crash after crash, and so near that the old mare would shudder and tremble under me, while the lightning seemed to leap from tree to tree. It was a most sublime spectacle, could one have been sheltered from the fury of the storm and felt himself safe and free from danger. The roaring of the wind, the waving of the trees, interlocking their branches with each other, the frequent crash of those thrown down by the force of the tempest and the vivid lightning, all combined, rendered the night terrific. Then a forked chain-like lightning in the distance, as the thunder cloud advanced, and the heavy reverberation of the distant thunder, intermixed with that near at hand, could not fail to impress with awe, if not terror, one of sterner stuff than myself. The rain raised some of the streams so that they were nearly impassable in the dark. I reached home about ten o'clock, drenched through and through, and nearly exhausted in holding the unbalanced load.

In 1797–8 or 9 (I think in '98) we had the most severe storm of thunder, lightning and rain, that I have ever known. The shower came from the west about five o'clock in the afternoon, and at its commencement was accompanied with wind and hail. It passed off to the east, and then the current of air seemed to change, which brought it back, so that it appeared as if two storms had met over head, to contend for mastery through the night; there was a continual flashing of lightning, and roar of thunder till daylight; much of it was in our immediate vicinity, and a large sugar maple was struck within a few rods of the house: the trunk was cleft in twain, so that it could be seen through its whole length though it remained standing till the next day, when it fell down. That storm extended all over the country and was long remembered. The June term of the common pleas was in session at Cooperstown, where the storm raged with equal fury as elsewhere; our large meadow was flooded with water nearly a foot deep. The Susquehanna river was so swollen, that a boy who was in the woods after cattle, was caught out, and remained in a tree top through the night, not deeming it safe to attempt to cross the river in the dark. The next morning he got across, by making an ox swim and he held by his tail, and was thus ferried over. . . .

An incident occurred in the early part of the storm, that I have just described, which deserves notice. Several neighbours as it came on took shelter in Mr. Edson's log-tavern, where there was a large stick chimney that admitted much hail and rain in the fire place and on the hearth. With the hail and rain that came pattering down, was a fish of the chub kind, about eight inches long, such as the boys used to catch with pin hooks in the brooks; he flopped about precisely as if thrown on land from the water, and was not injured; on being put in a pail of water, he swam about perfectly well. I have heard doubts expressed, whether fish are ever taken up, and then rained down, but I do not suppose there is any doubt about it; for what I have related I saw, and am sure the fish was not there by any other means. Water spouts at sea are familiar to all sailors, when vast columns of water are taken up, and no doubt fish with them, and are afterwards precipitated on the ocean, though of rare occurrence on land.

Let me leave this subject to relate a family incident, somewhat out of place but illustrative of the custom of the times: A few years after our settlement, a surveyor came there and was employed by my father and uncles to subdivide the lot, and run out and mark the lines of their respective farms; my father and three of his brothers were engaged, one carried the flag, two the chain, and the other an axe to clear away the brush, mark the line trees, and set and mark the corners.

On driving the last stake, and marking the witness trees of my father's farm, his brothers determined to whip him, to make him remember the corner; they prepared themselves with whips nearly as long and large as were used to drive oxen, and he procured one for defence equally as efficacious. To guard and prevent an attack from the rear, he placed his back against a large tree, which while it sheltered his back, warded off the blows they attempted to give him. They approached him in front, and he gave two of them each a hearty thwack across their shoulders and back, that raised ridges as large as the small finger, they struck at him but the tree warded off the force of their blows; and to bring the contest to a close, one of my uncles, a large strong man, more than six feet high, rushed in and grasping my father round the waist, threw him down, but he kept his whip, and gave them two more cuts after he was down. The contest ended, they got up, my uncles had the worst of it, for the whip had made a lively impression on the outer man; and my father had enough of it, to impress him forcibly with the remembrance of that corner. All was in good nature, regrets were expressed that either should have been hurt, the surveyor laughed, and the affair was settled.

As I am on incidents, let me relate another which happened a few years afterwards. We had a log school-house, near a pine swamp. It was sabbath day, and Parson Nash, afterwards, and for many years, favourably known as Father Nash, was to preach in the school-house. He was a pioneer in the new country, and I suppose is the Parson Grant, that Cooper had in his mind's eye, when he wrote *The Pioneers*. My father and a young man were going in the morning to build a fire in the school house, when they heard an outcry in the swamp of dogs and boys; presently a large bear came in sight, followed in close pursuit by two dogs, the one a large spirited animal fit for a fight, the other a yelping whiffit or fiste [a small mongrel] fit only to make a noise and pester an adversary. Two boys armed with clubs, who owned the dogs, and were following the bear, soon made their appearance. The dogs kept close to the bear, and would run up and snap his hinder parts, particularly when he clambered over logs, and as he turned to make fight or give them a slap, would break and fall back. They so annoyed him that he ran up several trees, but would come down in spite of the dogs, when the boys approached, and would shew his heels, the dogs constantly annoying him. My father armed himself with a club and joined in pursuit, sending back for his gun.

The messenger came, almost out of breath, and I followed him on his return. Bruin, in the meantime, hotly pursued, had treed several times, and would come down as before. The noise of the dogs, and shouts of the pursuers, brought my old grandfather, one of my uncles, and some others, with several strange dogs, into the swamp before the gun arrived. Bruin had gone up a large pine, and my father had reached the tree, and stood on one side, and my uncle, with an axe, on the other; the dogs were barking, and the bear looking down upon them. The large brindle dog, who first followed him, got into a fight with one of the others, and this bruin regarded as a favorable moment to attempt an escape; losing his hold, so as to slide down the tree, he came down stern foremost, almost as quick as his weight would have brought him had he fallen, making the bark fly, as he scraped his way down with his nails. He came on the side where my uncle stood with the axe, who gave him a large flesh wound, but it neither impaired his strength or disabled him from running. The axe, as it slipped from the bear, struck the brindle dog in the mouth, as he ran to seize him, and cut out two of his teeth. The bear was off, and the dogs at his heels so annoyed him, that he soon ran up another pine, where resting himself, with his neck partly over a limb, some fifty or sixty feet high, he watched the proceedings below.

The gun arrived, and was charged with pigeon or squirrel shot; for neither ball or buck shot were to be had. My father tore off a rag and wrapped in it as many shot as he could force down the barrel, intending to make a sort of cartridge, that should keep the shot more closely together, when they were discharged. This being done, and the priming being replenished with fresh powder, a short consultation was had, as to the best place to shoot the "varmint."

My father decided on shooting him in the throat, as he projected his head over the limb; and then the old patriarch, my grandfather, interposed his advice, with suggestions as to the beauty and importance of holding the gun steady, and making sure aim. It was well directed, and on being discharged, bruin tumbled to the ground; but with a skill, peculiar to the animal, fell like an old rug, apparently unhurt by the fall. He was up and off in a moment, followed by the dogs, yelling and yelping like so many fiends. The blood flowed copiously from the wound, like a stuck hog, so that it was apparent the shots had well performed their office. A run of twenty-five rods exhausted him, and he gave up. He was of the long legged brawny kind, large, though not very fat, but was well fitted for a fight or a race.

He was dragged out of the swamp, a team was sent for, and poor bruin was "toted" to Edson's log tavern, where the whole congregation, with Father Nash, assembled. Mr. Edson brought out his poor rum, gave the company a treat, himself included and the bear, having his skin pulled off, was soon turned into bear meat, and distributed. Father Nash ate of it at supper and made himself sick; the hunt had spoiled his forenoon services, for the bear had more attraction than the worthy parson. He, however, rather admitted that it was a good christian act to destroy the dangerous animal on the sabbath; and if not precisely within the canons of the church, the offence was venial, and should be overlooked.

It is wonderful how much a small resolute dog, that is fleet of foot, and understands his business, can annoy a bear. Neither a small or large dog should risk a fight, but by running up and snapping his hinder parts, and breaking and falling back, when the bear turns upon them, they soon pester him so that he takes to the tree.

A few years, after the incident just related, another bear, much larger and fatter than the former, was killed in the same swamp. He had been marauding the night before in a young orchard, regaling himself on sweet apples, of which the bear is very fond. He was encountered by a resolute bull dog, who was on the watch, and with the courage, for which his kind is distinguished, laid hold of bruin for a regular set-to; precisely what the bear wanted, for he fully comprehended that sport, and gave the dog a hug and a slap with his great paw and long nails, that knocked the old fellow over; inflicting wounds from which the bull dog never recovered. . . .

III

It is time to go back to more early incidents, than some of those related in the preceding chapter. Richfield when first organized as a town, comprised what is now Richfield, Plainfield, Exeter, and part of Winfield. In our part of it (the present town of Richfield) there were no residents when we went there, except a family or two, four miles east of us, who lived in a log house, on the Tunnicliff Farm, built before or immediately after the revolutionary war, near the present Richfield springs. There was no road or pathway between that settlement and ours; in passing from one place to the other, the marked trees on the line of lots were generally followed.

My father used to keep a lancet, with which he would open a vein, whenever it was necessary to let blood, for it was several years before we had a physician near us. If a tooth required to be extracted he had a primitive mode and quite effective. My uncle had a large double tooth that pained him excessively, so that he could have no rest day or night till it was removed. He came and said it must be drawn; and as there was no turn screw or other instrument for drawing teeth in the neighbourhood, a piece of hard seasoned wood was prepared to serve as a punch, and my uncle placing his head against the wall of the house, to keep it firm and steady, my father adjusting the punch against the offending tooth, gave it a smart blow with a hammer, loosening it from its socket, and then pulled it out with pincers.

Let me describe the first wedding, which was the marriage of a sister of my mother, who was married to Ebenezer Russell; the marriage was at my father's, in the log house; I do not remember how the parties were dressed, but no doubt in their best gear. Judge Cooper, of Cooperstown, was sent for, being the nearest magistrate, and came eighteen miles principally through the woods, to perform the ceremony. The neighbours were invited, the old pine table was in the middle of the room, on which I recollect was placed a large wooden bowl filled with fried cakes (nut cakes or dough nuts, as the country people call them). There might have been something else to constitute the marriage feast, but I do not recollect any thing except a black junk bottle filled with rum; some maple sugar, and water. The judge was in his long riding boots, covered with mud up to his knees, his horse was fed, that he might be off when the ceremony was over; the parties presented themselves, and were soon made man and wife as his "Honor" officially announced. He then gave the bride a good hearty kiss, or rather smack, remarking that he always claimed that as his fee; took a drink of rum, drank health, prosperity and long life to those married, ate a cake or two, declined staying even for supper, said he must be on his way home, and should go to the foot of the lake that night, refused any other fee for his services, mounted his horse and was off; and thus was the first marriage celebrated. The few other guests who were in attendance, remained and partook of as good a meal as the house could afford.

I may as well speak of the first death and funeral, that followed soon after, I think within a year. There had, to be sure, been a man killed, within the boundaries of the town, by the fall of a tree a short time before, but he was regarded as an itinerant, looking for land, rather than as an inhabitant of the town. My aunt, whose marriage I have just related, went into a consumption and died at my father's in the spring, soon after the leaves and flowers had put forth. A small elm stood by the brook near the house, on which a pair of yellow robins (Baltimore orioles) made a nest that year for the first time, and resorted there many succeeding years. The singing of that bird is sweet and plaintive, we all listened to it, and my mother and her poor sick sister, both strongly tinctured with Dutch superstitions, believed the bird to have come there to announce the death. . . .

During her sickness my father had provided some pine boards for a coffin, which after her death, he made himself and stained it black. The neighbors assembled; we had no clergyman, for at that day there was none in the vicinity; Timothy Hatch, father of Hon. Moses P. Hatch, of Oswego, read a chapter, and at the grave a hymn, "why do we mourn departing friends?" With these humble ceremonies the body was deposited in its "narrow house," then "earth to earth, ashes to ashes, dust to dust," were pronounced, a rough stone was planted at the head; and there the remains have rested for sixty years.

As I am on early incidents, let me refer to the organization of the county of Otsego, which was set off from Montgomery (formerly Tryon) in February, 1791. William Cooper was first judge, and Jedediah Peck was one of the judges. My father was made justice of the peace, at an early day after the county was organized. A day was agreed upon for all those appointed, to meet at Cooperstown to take the oath of office, and receive their commissions. My father got a new blue coat rather short, which was pronounced by a country tailor, "a handsome genteel coat." I recollect a rather coarse pair of white top'd boots for the occasion. At the appointed time he went, and I think walked there and back, which was as well as to ride, as the roads then were. He stayed all night, and with those that met there, must have had a hard time of it at Griffin's tavern, "the Bold Dragoon" of *The Pioneers,* for he came home lame, partly from an injury in a scuffle pulling off each other's boots *nolens volens*, and partly from walking so far in his new ones.

Among the justices was James Aplin, an honest, worthy but rather vain man, who lived in Hartwick. They used to tell this anecdote of him, but whether true or false I cannot state. It was said, that on his return home, he remarked to his better half, "My dear, last night you slept with James Aplin; to-night with James Aplin, esquire; God bless my good friend, Judge Cooper."

As Judge Cooper has been introduced, I may as well relate an incident witnessed by my father, not far from this time, and I am not sure but the very time he went to Cooperstown to receive his commission. I have thought it strange that James F. Cooper, the novelist, has not introduced it in some of his works, and once spoke to him about it and related the circumstances, as my father described them. A wrestling match was got up, in front of Griffin's; where a ring was formed, and the parties matched for the contest. Judge Cooper said he was a wrestler himself; and believed he could throw any man in the county; and further, that he wanted to find a man on his patent, who could throw him; remarking, that he would give any one in the company, one hundred acres of land, who would throw him at arms length. Timothy Morse, who I have elsewhere mentioned as a strong man, stepped up and laying his hands on the judge's shoulder, said, "Cooper, I believe I can lay you on your back." Cooper replied, "If you can I will give you one hundred acres." A ring was formed, and at it they went, and Morse soon brought him to the position indicated. The judge got up and ordered Richard Smith, his clerk, to make out the necessary papers for one hundred acres.

This Richard Smith was the first sheriff of the county. Whether a deed was executed for this one hundred acres, or the value of the land deducted from a previous or other purchase, I am not positive; but have always supposed Morse resided on the identical hundred acres in Burlington. There is no doubt, I presume of the wrestling match, and that one hundred acres was at stake; for the contest is still remembered by some of the old inhabitants, who point out the place where they wrestled, near the corner of the present Eagle tavern, formerly Griffin's.

When I mentioned this to James F. Cooper, he remarked "that it used to be fashionable to wrestle where his father was brought up, and from whence he removed to Otsego county; and that William Penn was a celebrated wrestler, and introduced and encouraged this with other athletic sports among his colonists."

It is generally known that a small portion of Otsego county was settled at a much earlier day than 1790. Cherry Valley was commenced about 1740 or '41, and when the Revolution broke out, contained a good number of inhabitants, who were generally of Scotch and Irish descent. In the north part of Springfield, a few Dutch families had settled, and at Unadilla, Butternuts, and present town of Otsego, a few English families had located before the war. But the great body of the county was a wilderness in 1790.

Samuel Crafts, esq. who has recently died in the town of Hartwick, a few miles from Cooperstown, at a very advanced age, came from Connecticut to Springfield, a few years after the war. He had been a Revolutionary soldier, and must have been nearly the first New Englander that came to the county; having arrived there several years before its organization. When Judge Cooper, the founder of Cooperstown, came, Capt. Crafts was living in Springfield, and conveyed the judge in a boat from the head of Otsego lake to its foot, where Cooperstown is situated.

Mr. Crafts was an industrious, worthy intelligent man; of stern, unbending integrity, and I think was a justice in the first commission of the peace; and foreman of the first grand jury in the county. He was father of Willard Crafts, esq., of Utica, a highly respectable citizen.

My readers may wish to know something more of our mode of life for the first few years, and what our provisions were. The mills were poor and flour consequently coarse and often black from smutty wheat. The Indian corn of course made good meal and johnny cakes, when ground, but as it would take two days at least to go and return from mill, many families had what they called a samp mortar; that is, a hard log with the end cut off square, set on end and hollowed out at top, as the Indians prepare theirs for the reception of corn, which is then pounded and broken by hand, with a pestle. . . .

I have had many a good supper of samp [corn mush] and milk, made in this way. The milk and butter were often disagreeable, from the cows eating the wild leeks and this, when used, was obviated by eating a piece of the same, which disguised the leeky taste of the milk and butter. We could always get fish, by going to the lake; and most generally brook trout, for several years, from the small streams, where none can be found at present.

I may as well remark, that when we first came to the country, it was said shad and herring annually came up the Susquehanna, to where mill-dams obstructed their ascent. As to fresh meat, we had it, as the Indian did his, whenever we could get it. Venison was quite common, bear meat occasionally, and perhaps veal three or four times a year, by dividing round and exchanging among our families; which including my grandfather in our circle, were five. When they had veal, a pot pie must always be made, and the whole tribe congregated to partake of it. There was but one iron pot in the settlement, which belonged to my grandfather, and this was sent to the house where the feast was to be provided. My grandmother always presided at the making of these pies, and she could make them better than any one I ever saw. The dough or paste was spread over and round the inside of the pot, before the meat was put in; and when done was called the crust. This would come out a little browned on the outside, but light and tender, not such heavy, clammy stuff, as is too often made now. When it was placed on the pine table, on a large pewter platter, it was very inviting, and delicious.

Good spring water was the beverage, each house being placed near a spring; for they had no wells, and if the springs failed in summer, they would clear them out, and dig deeper, or find a new one. They had no temperance societies, in those days; and no one, whether he drank or not, deemed it sinful or improper to refresh the inner man, when the needful could be had. After the first year, they generally had at their feasts a black junk bottle, that would hold a quart of rum, and this was dealt out in a wine glass; about half a gill to each man. Of course there was not much intemperance in town, till many years afterwards; and not very much then, or at any time.

Wild pigeons were plenty, spring and fall, and were killed and eaten in great numbers. The black and grey squirrel, it is known, hardly ever precede civilization, but follow it. We had been there several years before any were seen. Foxes also generally follow instead of preceding. Martens, or as the Indians call them "wau-pau-nau-cau," were quite plenty, and occasionally an otter, in the larger streams.

I must say something about schools. My father had learned me my letters some time before we had a school, and I could spell ba, and soon after baker. I remember his first teaching me my letters. There was A, with two feet, i with a dot, round O, Q with a tail, crooked S, T with a hat, &c. &c. After six or seven families had settled within striking distance, it was decided that a school house must be built, and a summer school started for the children. The house must be near water, and must be built where it would best accommodate its patrons; accordingly a place was selected, the neighbours made a bee, came together, cut away the underbrush, and the trees, that were near enough to endanger the house. They cut logs, drew them to the place, and put up a log house, small but low, and the roof nearly flat for several years; and covered with bark. One side was so much elevated by an additional log, that the water would run off, and subsequently rafters were added, making an ordinary roof, but no floor over head. The floor beneath was made of split logs, hewed to make them smooth; and some narrow benches made from split logs, supported by legs, were put in for the scholars. There were no writing tables or desks, but these were added afterwards when they wanted to educate larger boys, and were made by boring into the logs, and driving pins to support a sloping board for a writing table, so that those who wrote sat with their faces to the wall, and their backs to the teacher.

There was no glass to be had for windows in the country, and, as a substitute, a rude sash was made and placed in the wall, and this sash was supplied with white paper, which being oiled or greased, would let in the light and exclude the wind. When the weather became cold, a large fire place and stick chimney, daubed with mud, were added, and this was the first school house in that part of the county. A school was kept for several summers by a schoolmistress, who boarded round among the proprietors, and in the winter by schoolmasters, when the larger boys attended. To this school house, scholars were sent from abroad [*i.e.*, other communities, where there were no schools], who boarded with the proprietors.

The boarding of the schoolmistress and master always led to one agreeable result. The family lived better, and had more of the delicacies and luxuries of life, than on ordinary occasions. This rendered boarding round popular, among the children at least; for preparatory to the master or mistress coming, an additional quantity of fried cakes must be prepared, and mince and other pies, if they could be afforded. In truth, the master and mistress were regarded as distinguished personages. This first house was used for several years, when it was deemed advisable to build another, further south, to accommodate those living in that direction.

The second one, was a little south of the orchard, now on the farm formerly owned by my father, and it was in this building, that father Nash was to preach when the bear was killed. The schoolboy pranks were rude and abundant, as they are at all schools.

The day the second house was completed we had some cider brought there, to dedicate the house, being the first I had ever tasted, and the first ever brought into that part of the town; the cider having been brought there by some one from Cherry Valley or Mohawk river. The snows fell deep every winter; the boys used to wrestle and wallow in the snow, and often fight; then, if the master found it out, they were almost sure to be flogged, for the birch and ferule were regarded, in those days, as indispensable appendages; and by frequent appliances "the young idea was taught to shoot." In winter, all the children were clothed with coarse thick home made clothing; they brought their dinner with them to school, and after eating it indulged in play of course.

Those narrow benches were awfully tiresome. Children

would get tired and sleepy, but their vigilant instructors would contrive to stir them up; sometimes by one, and then by other devices.

The children were of course restless, and wanted to go out, which they were permitted to do, once each half day, and oftener by special permission. Sometimes the instructor so arranged matters in relation to going out, that any one might enjoy that privilege as a matter of course, each half day, without asking, provided he could go alone, when all others were in school. To carry out this provision, a hole was bored in one of the logs of the house, in which a loose wooden peg was inserted, which any one might take as a passport out of the house; and when he had stayed the permitted time, he returned and placed the peg in position, which might be taken by another without applying to the master, and thus disturbing the school.

The boys were taught by their instructors how to make their best bow, and how to address strangers in the most formal style; and the girls how to shew off their graces, by the most fashionable curtsies.

Better progress was made in education than could have been expected, and nearly all of mine was obtained in such schools as I have described. I could always read and spell as well, and I thought a little better than any in school, and when put to my arithmetic, went directly ahead of all competitors. I could play as well as any one; run much better on the snow crust than most of them; always fond of play and frolic; and never doubted but what I could do anything that others could. This impression has been a leading one through life, and to my perseverance in it, I have ascribed much of my success. That I could not do a thing, that wanted doing, never entered my mind. In the winter nearly all the boys went to school, and in the summer, those large enough to work, staid at home and worked on the farm; going barefoot till cold weather came again. This going barefoot in a new country, among small stumps and roots, is a bad business. The feet get sore, and then to go in the woods among the ground yew, was exceedingly annoying to sore feet. It was however the fashion of the country and could not be avoided; for shoes were not to be had, except for winter, when a "cat whipper" came to the family, with kit, and made them.

The sugar-making session was always hailed with rapture by the boys. No one, brought up in a new country, but can realize how exciting it was, and how eager and industrious the boys were to commence tapping the trees. This used to be done by cutting a notch in the sugar maple, and putting a spout under it; inserted by driving in a partly rounded, sharp iron instrument, called a tapping gouge, to cut a place for the spout that led the sap to the trough. Sap buckets were not then introduced, nor did they use an auger, as they do now, for tapping trees.

Troughs were generally made from the butternut, and would hold about a pailful, and some nearly two. The season having arrived, boys with their hand sleds would soon distribute the troughs to the trees that were to be tapped, by drawing them in the morning on the snow crust. Then the master of ceremony would follow with his axe, spouts, and tapping gouge; the sharp ringing of the iron, as he drove the gouge into the tree, kept all advised where he was. The trees being tapped and troughs set, the next thing was to shovel away the snow, and prepare a place to hang the kettles for boiling.

I have frequently found the ground covered two or three feet deep with snow, entirely free from frost, and the young leeks already pricking up through the ground and reaching the snow that lay on it. The gathering of sap, which had to be done generally with pails, was hard work while the snow lasted, as we frequently sunk into

the snow up to our knees. When the boiling was commenced, a small piece of pork was thrown in the kettle, to
prevent the sap, as it boiled, from running over. The little
chickadee birds are always attracted to where one is at
work in the woods, and they would generally find the
spare piece of pork and pick and eat it up, unless concealed. The sugaring off, gave great delight to the parties
present, as every one knows; and this sugar making, in a
new country, is always to boys a delightful employment.
When we had a good run of sap, as it was called, that is,
when it ran freely, I have frequently remained in camp,
and tended the kettles late in the evening. The atmosphere being clear and delightful in spring time, the drop-
ping of the sap in the troughs could be heard in all direc-
tions; and for a considerable distance; and then the
hooting and screaming of owls, often very near, being attracted by the fire, would, to an unpractised ear, render
night hideous, discordant and melancholy.

Before passing to other matters, I may as well mention
a little incident illustrative of the hardships and hardihood of life in a new country. We had been some two or
three years at our new home, when it seemed to be necessary for some one to return to our former residence in
Rensselaer county. The principal object was to collect in
some small debts, and to adjust some unsettled matters.
My mother wanted to go and visit her parents and relatives
in Cambridge, Washington county, so she concluded to
make the visit, and then go to Hoosic on business matters.
One, and I am not sure but two, of my uncles, were going
the same time to arrange their affairs, so my mother was
to go with them. They were all to go on horseback, and
my mother for want of a better, was to ride on a man's
saddle. We had a high-spirited black horse, which she was
to ride; a pillow was strapped on the saddle, saddle bags or
portmanteaus properly adjusted, and thus rigged and

equipped, she started off with my uncles; I think it was in the fall of 1792, and I am quite sure she carried a child. They were to strike the Mohawk river at Canajoharie, then across the country to Johnstown and Saratoga, and thence to Cambridge.

I remember how they looked as they started off. As soon as they had crossed a small pole bridge, near the house, my mother to show her fearlessness, and that she could control her horse, gave him a slight blow, that put him into a good round gallop, and they were soon out of sight, as they rode along the narrow, crooked pathway through the woods. She returned in due time, having made the journey comfortably, had a good visit, and transacted the business correctly. Every woman in a new country soon becomes a fearless rider. It is a noble and invigorating exercise, and a woman never appears so well as when she is well mounted, on a spirited horse. This was the most fashionable mode of travelling in that part of the country for many years afterwards. Even as late as 1806–7, young people when they went to a ball, or fashionable party, generally went on horseback. It is so yet in the new States at the west. . . . Judge Cooper had a favourite daughter killed by a fall from a starting horse, as she was going to the town of Butternuts, at a very early day after the settlement of the county.

I must say something about the scarcity of books, and the difficulty of obtaining anything like readable matter, except the Bible, psalm book, and a few other books, till we had been several years in the county. Each family had a Bible and psalm book; my grandfather had a large English Bible with the liturgy, and versification of the psalms, as used by the English church. The Bible was printed, the old testament at Oxford, and the new testament at London in 1715. He also had a copy of *Hudibras,* which next to the Bible, he regarded as superior to all other productions. My father had two volumes of Dryden's poems; and one of my uncles a copy of Young's *Night Thoughts*. This was about all the reading matter for four or five families in our circle, till a small town library was established a few years afterwards. After learning to read, I went through with the books I have mentioned, and could soon repeat a great number of psalms and hymns, and a large portion of *Hudibras*, as I can to this day. The library being established, was kept about two miles from my father's. The books were drawn out, and returned once a month. To encourage me to read he very soon after its establishment, used to send me to return the books, and draw new ones, directing me to select according to my choice. I used to read all that were drawn out, and among others I recollect reading six volumes of Bruce's *Travels to [Discover] the Sources of the Nile*. Grecian and Roman history became familiar to me; superficially to be sure, but more in detail and incident than I now recollect them.

That old library was added to, and kept up till after I left Richfield, in 1810; and I have always thought, and have no doubt, that it induced a propensity for reading among the farmers, that for many years put them ahead for general intelligence, of those in other towns where a library was neglected. In imitation of this library among the men, I set on foot a project for a library among the boys, and we got up quite a respectable juvenile library, which ran down about 1805, in consequence of our treasurer and librarian misapplying the funds.

I do not remember how many years it was after the first settlement, before we had a mail in that part of the county, but should think six or seven years, and probably more; newspapers were scarce. The *Otsego Herald*, a very small weekly paper, was published by Judge Phinney and continued for many years; this was almost the only paper that any citizen in town had an opportunity of reading. It was sometimes brought by a post rider; and at other times a class of thirteen was formed, each member going to Cooperstown for the papers once a quarter. The motto of the *Herald* was kept up as long as it was published,

> "Historic truth our Herald shall proclaim,
> The law our guide, the public good our aim."

With the almost surfeit of newspapers that we now have, it is difficult to imagine with what avidity the little weekly messenger was sought after, and how thoroughly it was read among the neighbours.

At an early day after I was able to read, my father to encourage me, used to buy small books, and among those was a little one, giving an account of the trial and execution of the King and Queen of France, illustrated with an engraving, shewing the guillotine, and Gen. Santerre, mounted on a large horse, with troops under arms. The reading of this book, with occasional scraps from newspapers, excited an eager desire to make myself acquainted with the important events growing out of the French revolution. I have a slight recollection of the siege of Toulon in 1794, when Buonaparte first distinguished himself in driving off the English. The campaigns of 1795 I recollect, the most of them from newspaper readings. Buonaparte's Italian campaign in 1796, and from that time till his final downfall and banishment to St. Helena, all the principal events are more firmly fixed in my memory than occurrences of a recent date.

In 1797–8–9, the *Otsego Herald*, was generally brought by a post rider, who left our paper each Saturday afternoon at a neighbour's about a mile off; and it was my business to run through the woods over a hill (often before breakfast) after the paper, and I generally read the part containing the news, before reaching home. The escape and sailing of the French fleet from Toulon in 1798, with the army for the Egyptian expedition; the pursuit by Nelson in search of it, created a deep sensation in this country, for several months before hearing of the landing in Egypt, and destruction of the French fleet at the battle of the Nile. It must be recollected that in 1798, our troubles with the French Republic had assumed a belligerent aspect, almost a declaration of war on each side.

The object of the expedition was secret, and many apprehended an invasion from this formidable army, with Buonaparte at its head; at last the expedition was heard from, by its attack and conquest of Malta. Next came the battle of the Nile in large capitals, with Nelson's official account from the Vanguard, off the mouth of the Nile, &c. The contest that we had with the French kept up an interest. Truxton captured Le Insurgent, of superior force. Bainbridge, Tingey, Talbot and others distinguished themselves. I recollect a doggerel song got up and published in the *Herald,* about that time. Let me give you a stanza or two, to call up old recollections.

> "Of our tars so brave and handy,
> Gallant Truxton is the dandy,
> Talbot, Bainbridge, Morris too
> Are among the valiant crew.
>
> They're a match for hostile dogs, sir,
> Whether they eat beef or frogs, sir,
> Let them meet by night or day,
> They will shew them Yankee play."

Several other patriotic effusions appeared from week to week in the *Herald,* which as they bring up old matters may now be inserted and not deemed out of place.

"I wonder what the matter means,
    A cutting of such capers,
The parson says the French are mad,
    He reads it in the papers,

Hey ho Billy bo, I b'lieve the wars are coming,
And if they do, I'll get a gun as soon as I hear them
    drumming.

I heard them say on training day,
    That Washington's a-going,
And Captain Toby swears they'l fall,
    Like grass when he's a mowing,

Hey ho, &c.

He says as how in t'other war,
    He ran right at the bullets,
And never minded grenadiers,
    No more than we do pullets."

Hey ho, &c.

Another.

"There's Yankee doodle come to town,
    From Philadelphia city,
He's ranged the streets all up and down,
    And brought nice news to fit ye.

He's been among the Peeplish folks,
    And vows they're rotten clever,
They talk so 'cute and crack such jokes,
    Would make one stare for ever."

Soon afterwards the *Herald* was dressed in mourning on the death of the father of his country, George Washington, who died in December, 1799. The announcement of which melancholy event threw the whole country in consternation and sorrow. We had an assemblage, and a funeral oration from our singing master Doctor Meacham, who stood on the table in Brewster's ball room. I have recently seen a piece of mourning drapery from the Otsego Lodge, Cooperstown, used on that occasion.

In the *Herald* and other papers, a discussion was kept up, whether the nineteenth century commenced 1st January 1800, or 1801; very similar to the recent discussion in regard to the commencement of the present last half century. I do not recollect which side Judge Phinney took, but I think in favor of 1801. Peter Porcupine had illustrated his views of the question, by comparing mile stones to centuries; and had asserted that any one differing from his position, had no more brains than an oyster. In a new year's address probably written by Judge Phinney, was this verse,

> "This good day my friends will enter ye,
> Fairly in the nineteenth century,
> In spite of mile stones on the plains,
> In spite of Peter's oyster brains."

At the age of fifteen I had become a large stout boy, worked hard on the farm all the year, except about four months in winter, when I went to school. From the age of ten years, I used to go to mill on horseback, often ten miles or more, which of course brought me in contact with other boys, who came many miles on the same business. Our casual interviews were not of the most amicable character, they often assumed a belligerent aspect, and not unfrequently bloody noses grew out of them. On one occasion, a boy a year older and much larger than myself, became insolent, and after threatening to lick me, persisted in fastening his quarrel so that I could not avoid a set-to. The miller wanting to see the sport encouraged it, and the result was my adversary was essentially flogged within three minutes, and came out of the contest with his nasal organ pretty well swollen and bleeding freely, while my face was only slightly scratched, but not hurt.

Many similar incidents occurred with the Dutch boys during these excursions to mill, who were very much inclined to flog the "Yankees," as they called us. So also at school such frolics were not unusual, as well as playing off divers pranks on those who were regarded as rather soft and green. My friend, Samuel Russell, was generally in concert with me, and was not only fond of fun, but full of school boy pranks in the superlative degree. A negro who used to go to school, was frequently duped and made the laughing stock of the company. On one occasion we made him believe he could fly, and persuaded him to jump from the highest part of a shed, some fourteen feet to the frozen ground. He went up, and after flopping and swinging his arms as a rooster does his wings, crowed stoutly, and then leaped off, intending to fly and come down lightly, but his avoirdupoise brought him to the frozen ground with a violence that nearly broke his limbs. On another occasion, we persuaded him to dive from a high stump, into what he thought was a bank of light snow recently fallen, but which in fact was a knoll slightly covered; much of the new snow having been blown off. Ike, for that was the negro's name, went in head foremost, and although it of course did not hurt his head, it nearly broke his neck, for he complained for a long time of the injury. After these adventures he was more cautious, but was still the dupe of his tormentors, who frequently got him into other scrapes, such as only could be tolerated as boyish pranks, or as another has fitly, said, "youthful indiscretions."

Russell has been prosperous in life, and though starting

poor and entirely destitute, is not only comfortably off in regard to property, but a correct business man. He has represented Otsego county in the assembly; has been commissioner of loans and county clerk; and now possesses, in an eminent degree, the confidence and respect of his neighbours and friends. I must relate an ancedote of his father, an old revolutionary soldier, who I remember seeing nearly fifty-seven years ago. The old man thought he was somewhat religious, and probably was, though it was not that strait laced religion that would preclude him from cracking his jokes and enjoying his fun, of which he was as fond as his son. On one occasion he was attending a conference meeting, when an aged sister, whom Russell disliked excessively, got up, and addressing the meetiing with a decided nasal twang, said "My dear brothers and sisters, I feel like a poor miserable creature," and sat down. Capt. Russell immediately arose and said, "I can fellowship you in *that*, for I think you are," and then took his seat. Some of those in attendance laughing, and others suppressing a desire to laugh, at the old man's prompt and appropriate response.

I ought to say something about our spiritual teachers. We had quacks, and empyrics in divinity, as well as in physic, during the early days of our new residence. Many straggling itinerants came among us and would give the neighbours what was called a sermon, which might have been called anything else just as well. There was one man, who for several years gave us the "stated preaching of the gospel." He was a Rhode Island farmer, of the Baptist denomination, very illiterate, and known all over the country, as "old esq. Pray."

He owned a fine farm on the Unadilla river, in the present town of Winfield, and kept a poor tavern, where he sold most villainous New England rum. Elder Pray had his farm carried on, but did not work much himself, generally staying in the house to tend bar and see to matters relating to his tavern. On Sunday he would ride away in pursuance of previous appointments, and preach, as he called it.

His education was so defective that he could hardly read his Bible intelligibly; and his preaching, if possible, was more defective still. He used the most unsavory similes to illustrate his positions. I heard him, on one occasion, describe the operations of the Holy Spirit; and to show how inadequate human means were, to promote the new birth, he illustrated his views, by introducing as a simile, a carved basswood woman, and then went on with his comparison, altogether too indecent to repeat. It answered however for preaching, for want of better.

Jedediah Peck, the indomitable democrat, who soon after the organization of the county, got up an opposition to Judge Cooper, Genl. Morris, and the federal party generally, was a preacher as well as politician. He was illiterate, but a shrewd cunning man. For many years he controlled the politics of the county, put up and put down who he pleased; he had no talent as a preacher or speaker; his language was low, and he spoke with a drawling, nasal, yankee twang, so that in public speaking he was almost unintelligible. He always had his saddle bags with him, filled with political papers and scraps, that he distributed whenever he went from home, and then at night and frequently on Sundays, would hold meeting and preach.

I have always been so uncharitable as to believe his preaching resulted more from a desire to promote political than spiritual objects. Still the judge was a worthy, honest, exemplary man; and was entitled to great credit. He represented the county many years in the assembly and senate; and had as much influence, and I think more than any county member. It was through his exertions the foundation of our school fund was laid; and for that act alone, if for no other, he is entitled to the gratitude of the state. [Peck is properly remembered as father of the public school system in New York State.] He was county judge for many years, and in 1812, although of advanced age, was in Queenstown battle, acting as paymaster of Col. Stranahan's regiment. The old man of nearly seventy years crossed the river and behaved remarkably well. The official account of the battle made honorable mention of him.

The Federalists disliked the judge, and always ridiculed him and his decisions in court. Not being a lawyer by profession, his honor never pretended to much knowledge of the law, but went for the common sense, reasonable construction of each transaction. I recollect a case of crim. con. [adultery], when he charged the jury. The defendant attempted to show that the plaintiff knew of and colluded at the transgression of his wife; this, if true, would have been a good legal defence. Not establishing this point, as he intended, he next resorted to proof in mitigation of damages, and proved the wife not only abandoned, but of infamous reputation; this, the books all agree, should be taken into consideration in fixing the amount of damages.

His honor however decided and charged the jury, that it was neither a justification or mitigation, but on the contrary, a gross aggravation, which ought to enhance the damages against defendant, for having anything to do with the dirty slut. Not very sound law to be sure, but well enough for such a suit.

For several years very few incidents occurred worthy of record; suffice it to say, I worked hard all the year, except winter, when I went to school. In this way I became familiar with all kinds of work incident to a new country, and on arriving at twenty-one years of age, was a good practical farmer.

I recollect in 1801–2 or 3, when I must have been some fifteen, sixteen, or seventeen years old, of assisting my father in cutting down and sawing into logs, the largest and tallest wild (black) cherry tree that I ever saw. It seems to me it was very near three feet in diameter, and held nearly that size the whole length of its trunk; it was perfectly straight, and we cut from it five or six logs, twelve feet long, before reaching a limb. The logs were cut by a cross cut saw, and I know it was while I was a mere boy, as it fatigued me very much to carry my end of it while we were cutting them.

My father was preparing to build a house, and he wanted the boards and timber from this tree to use about the house, and for making cherry furniture. We cut it two or three years before it was to be used, that it might be well seasoned. I speak particularly of this tree, because from some of its boards, in 1805, was made the case for that old family clock, that I have had long before the remembrance of either of my children. Soon after the falling of that tree, a young one shot up from or among its roots, and was protected by the stump of the parent tree for many years. We preserved it, and if still standing, as I suppose it is, may be seen very near the southerly line of the large orchard, planted on my father's farm. That young tree must be about fifty years old, and I suppose two feet in diameter. . . .

I ought to mention among these old recollections, my first visit to Albany [a distance of 70 miles], at a very early day, and several years before the present century. I went there with my father on a load of wheat, by sleighing; we started very early in the morning, which was the fashion of those going to Albany, or they could not get back within five days, which was the usual time for a journey to the city and home again. It was a curious sight to observe the immense number of sleighs, on approach-

ing the city; a string a mile long, was no uncommon occurrence in those days, and even more. Generally speaking, each teamster carried his own hay, bound on to the
sleigh, with a bag or two of oats; he also had a pail or box
of provisions, and always a bottle of rum stowed away
among the bags of grain.

The fashion was to stop about once in ten miles, to feed
and rest the horses, and while they were eating their oats,
the owner felt bound to call for at least a mug of gingered
cider, or gill of rum, which served as a remuneration for
the use of the shed. At night he fed on his own provision,
but generally paid sixpence for a cup of tea or a like sum
for a mug of cider, and the same for his bed. For his
horses when he fed his own hay and grain, he paid sixpence or a shilling, and he took care of them himself; and
at these prices, William McKown, and others, who kept
taverns for the farmers, got rich. Those were good jolly
times; and if not rich and prosperous to those who thus
visited Albany, they could not well fail to be interesting,
for they brought citizens in contact, who lived remote
from each other.

I recollect the old Dutch church which I saw at this my
first visit, which stood at the foot of State street, very near
the exchange building in Albany. The venerable edifice
protected an old woman, who sold coffee and chocolate on
the south side, and sometimes "strong beer," as it was
called. My father patronized her, and bought a cup of the
former, and a glass of the latter, which was the first beer I
had ever tasted. I recollect very well the appearance of
the old church and of those sheltered on the south side,
which I have since seen coarsely delineated in print. We
of course went to see the lion that was kept somewhere on
the hill; but father did not go to see the Albany witch,
who was generally visited by those going there from the
country, who wanted to know their fortune, and who de-

lighted in the marvellous; which my father did not, for he was a perfect infidel, in relation to those matters. The witch made her craft a regular business at that time.

How interesting were those journeys to Albany, which from Richfield took about five days, and the usual load for a sleigh did not then exceed from twenty to twenty-five bushels, for the turnpike was not constructed. My father at this time received $1.68 per bushel for his wheat.

Those large winter fires at the taverns were delightful; and then the jingling of bells made travelling exceedingly spirited and cheerful. I went to Albany in 1811 or 1812, with Colonel Fitch and Captain Loomis, of Richfield, who were going with their wives; each had a sleigh pretty well loaded with country products, and each had a pail or box of excellent provisions ready cooked; they insisted on my going with them, and said it should not cost me a cent.

We had a pleasant journey to and from the city, and while there visited the Otsego members, who were stowed away in a small room, an upper story of a poor wooden building. How different from accommodations furnished the present members of the legislature, who have, gener- ally, pleasant respectable rooms, and good comfortable living, if nothing more.

IV

On arriving at eighteen years of age, I enrolled myself in a company of light infantry, commanded by Capt. Minerva Cushman, a worthy excellent man, who was father of Don F. Cushman, esq. a highly respectable and successful merchant of New-York, now doing business in Cortland street. This was one of the oldest independent companies in the county. In the autumn of 1805, our company, in common with the Otsego brigade, repaired to Cooperstown for parade, inspection and general review, in conformity to orders from Governor Lewis.

The governor was there with his staff, in full uniform; and I suppose was much gratified with the parade as well as his reception in the county. He was fond of show, and it was agreed by his opponents, that he was excessively vain in reference to military matters. Those brigade parades that he ordered, were not well received by the public; they required a sacrifice of three days time to a large portion of those subject to duty, and of course were attended with considerable expence. When brought forward as a candidate for re-election, these parades were urged against him with much effect.

In Otsego there was another matter of complaint that lost him some votes. Benjamin [*sic.* error for Stephen] Arnold, a schoolmaster, had whipped a little girl in an unmerciful manner, which caused her death; and the circumstances were such, that he was convicted of murder and sentenced for execution. On the day appointed, everybody repaired to Cooperstown to see Arnold hung. A gallows was erected, the prisoner was brought out and placed on the staging, where the sheriff with his deputies were in attendance. Clergymen were there, and went through with their religious exercises; the criminal was exhorted to make his everlasting peace, and the spectators to take warning and profit from the melancholy exhibition. Arnold was invited to address the multitude, which he did in a few words, but in so low a tone of voice as scarcely to be heard. He stood under the gallows, with the halter about his neck, expecting, as did those who were looking at him, that the next moment would be his last; when the sheriff put an end to the painful suspence, by taking from his pocket a commutation of the death penalty to imprisonment for life.

Arnold fainted on the annunciation, and the spectators were sadly disappointed. They were not slow in giving utterance to their feelings; some swore, others laughed, but all were dissatisfied. Many had come a great distance, their curiosity had been much excited, a day had been lost, besides incurring considerable expence, for which they had no corresponding return. The greater part wanted to see a man hung; and when Arnold was excused from gratifying their morbid desire, they acted and talked as if they must have a substitute. Had the governor himself been there, many of them would hardly have refrained from making him a conspicuous figure in the very interesting exhibition.

They had a right to be displeased; for if the sheriff was in possession of the governor's commutation, before Arnold was taken from jail, it was a wanton, inexcusable act of cruelty thus to expose him, and horrify his feelings; and it was so regarded by the bystanders, who thought the public exposure of the criminal should have been spared. I do not know what explanation could have been given; some said the messenger did not arrive with the commutation till just as the sheriff was preparing to swing up the prisoner; others said he had received it in due time, but wanted to make a show and frighten the culprit. I have no doubt the governor lost votes for his interference, if not for the circumstances at the gallows. . . .

Dancing has been a favorite amusement in all countries, and in all ages of the world. In the new settlements it was not so fashionable as more athletic exercises. For several years they had no suitable rooms; and then again, the farmers were staid in their habits, and generally had no desire to encourage it.

Those split logs from which the floors for houses were made, were not very well adapted for showing off the graces of motion. . . . Although we had dancing parties occasionally for several years, yet we did not have a dancing school in that part of Otsego county, till the winter of 1805 or 1806. A strolling dancing master then came there, and after much opposition from the serious part of the community, got up a class, and instructed them in jigs, French fours, and figures, throughout the winter. I was permitted to make one of the class, though my grandparents regarded it as a great scandal, and little better than serving the devil; they were probably about half right. We never aspired to cotillions; and I don't know but our light heeled instructor might have deemed himself incompetent to impart instruction beyond the first rudiments: "down the outside, up again; turn your partner; down in the middle, up again; cast off; and right and left."

We had no aristocracy in those days. The laboring man, who worked by the month, and the spinning girl who worked by the week, were as good as others, and of course must not be slighted, or overlooked. Dressed in their Sunday clothes they appeared well, and were respected. This was right. All were workers; and hard labor brought all on a level of equality.

I remember one of the early settlers, who is still living, and is now a wealthy farmer; who, when he came there had scarcely anything but his axe, and used to chop, and clear land by the acre, till he had earned enough to buy a new farm. On getting married, he was so determined not to disguise his condition in life, that he insisted on being married in the dress in which he expected to earn his living. The result was, that he dressed himself in a clean tow shirt, frock, and trowsers; while his wife, the daughter of a respectable farmer, put on her petticoat and short gown; and in these every-day dresses they were married.

It was no uncommon thing then, for the daughters of substantial farmers, to go out to work by the week, when they could be spared from home. Such a thing now is hardly thought of by our native-born citizens; in which respect I think they manifest a greater degree of false pride than good sense.

As I have referred to dancing; let me describe the arrangements for getting up a ball. The managers being chosen, had two ways of getting it up. One was to make a hap-hazard business, and let each gentleman to select his partner, and wait on her to the dance. When this mode prevailed, there was a scramble among the beaux to get the start of each other, to invite the young ladies who were regarded as favorites. This mode had its objections, as it not only induced scrambles, and competitions, but frequently resulted in leaving some of the girls less attractive at home, who would be overlooked. There was another objection that had weight, particularly with those young men who were admitted into society, not because their company was very desirable, but because it was an unpleasant business to exclude them. They were rather cheap, ordinary, or as the Buck Eyes would say, "or'nary fellows," who were sometimes refused by the ladies, because they of course had preferences, and would give these fellows "the mitten," and take their chance of an invitation from some one else. I presume my readers, particularly of the younger class, will understand what "giving the mitten" means. At any rate, those who were so unfortunate as to submit to that mortification, understood the meaning and preferred the other mode; because, as will soon be seen, they were backed up by the influence of the managers when the fair ones were invited. To obviate these objections, it was more generally voted that the other mode should be adopted, and that the managers should classify and select partners among the gentlemen and ladies. Preparatory to this important matter, lists were made out of those who were to be invited, and then the managers went to work and would set down Mr. A. B. and Miss C. D., and so on through the lists. Tickets were given out something in this form, "Independence Ball, Mr. A. B. is invited to attend a fourth of July ball, at &c. and to wait on Miss C. D., who is also invited." On receiving the ticket, the gentleman must call on the lady for whom a ticket was enclosed, and invite her attendance; which, under this arrangement, she almost invariably accepted; because to refuse would not only have been an insult to the gentleman, but to the managers who had selected, and by their ticket invited her; and they represented society, so that she would probably be excluded, unless she had good reasons for refusing. If it was a fourth of July ball, they frequently met before dinner, danced a few figures and then dined in the open air, under booths. After dinner they went to dancing in good earnest; had tea, cakes, and wine handed round at evening, and during the night; and frequently more stimulating potations, particularly among the gentlemen. They were not nice in the observance of hours, but danced them away till they were generally satisfied to break up at broad day light.

If it was a winter frolic they went in sleighs; but at other times, nearly all on horseback. The young gentleman would provide himself with as good a horse as he could, and another with a ladies saddle, for his partner. Thus furnished with the means of locomotion, he would start after the fair one, leading the horse she was to ride; and being equipped, girled, and mounted, they would start for the ball. As all were fearless riders, the horses were frequently put to the top of their speed. It was no uncommon thing for a young lady to mount the same horse behind the gentleman, and thus ride double to the ball.

The objection to the managers selecting and arranging was that they generally secured the lion's share for themselves, by selecting the favorite girls. They had the trouble of arranging for the ball; and I don't know that there was any violation of principle, if the managers did choose wisely. Some however did think it was objectionable, as they thought it conceded too much, and gave undue advantages to monopolise the choice articles. For several years we had no musician near us, and a committee had to be appointed to secure a fiddler from abroad. My first acquaintance with Brayton Allen, who played the violin remarkably well, was his attendance at Richfield to discourse eloquent music for a new year's ball. He then resided at Cherry Valley; has since resided in Western Virginia, on the great Kanawha, was always fond of fun and frolic, sang a good song, told a good story, was an accomplished shot, kept excellent hounds; a man of sense and sound philosophy, for he took the world easy, laughed at its follies, submitted to its crosses, and murmured not as its reverses. We have formerly ran down and unearthed many foxes; but for several years I have lost sight of him, and whether dead or alive, I really do not know. The fashions, in social life, have very much changed within the last forty or fifty years.

Now, when a party meet, and wish to take a social glass, a brandy smash or whisky toddy is prepared for each. Then, on meeting at a country tavern, some one of the company would call for a brandy sling, or a rum or gin sling, which required a gill of liquor; this being properly mixed, with sugar and water, and stirred up with the toddy stick, till the compound almost foamed, was ready for a sprinkling of nutmeg, and was then handed to the one who called for it. He took a drink and handed it to his neighbour; who drank and passed it along till it was drank off, and the one who finished it called for another, each one generally calling for a sling before the sitting was completed.

In reference to musicians, it has been above remarked, that they were scarce. I will relate a trifling incident, growing out of a performance on the violin, though not immediately connected with the thread of my story. Major [James] Cochran, who recently died at Oswego (universally esteemed and regretted, and whose excellent lady resides there still) could in his younger days play the fiddle. About the year 1796 he was a candidate for Congress against Judge Cooper, of Cooperstown. The congressional district embraced not only Montgomery and Otsego, the residences of Cochran and Cooper, but nearly the whole of western New York. After Major Cochran was put in nomination, he had occasion to visit the western counties and took his violin with him.

He stayed over night at Canandaigua, where a dance was got up, and the Major obliged and amused the company by fiddling for them. He beat Judge Cooper at the election, but whether from the influence of music and dancing or other causes, is now too late to enquire. It was alleged however that Judge Cooper had either published or remarked that Cochran had been through the district with his violin, and had fiddled himself into office. This came to Cochran's ear and brought him from Montgomery county to Cooperstown.

He started on horseback, as I have heard him say, and went there, where Judge Cooper was presiding as first judge at the court of Common Pleas. On his coming out of court Cochran met him, and after alluding to the election and what had taken place, informed the judge that he had come from the Mohawk to chastise him for the insult.

Judge Cooper treated it lightly, and remarked that Cochran could not be in earnest, who answered by a cut with his cow skin [whip]. Cooper closed in with his adversary, but Cochran being a large strong man, they were pretty well matched for the scuffle, and the judge did not throw him down as he intended; the by-standers interposed and the parties were separated. Cochran was indicted for the assault and battery, but removed the indictment to the [court of] oyer and terminer, where he pleaded guilty, and was fined a small amount for the breach of the peace. How it happened that they were opposing candidates, I really do not know; they were both Federalists, and I am quite sure both belonged to the same party at that time. Major Cochran has told me that he supported John Adams' administration, and was always regarded as an out-and-out old fashioned Federalist.

Judge Cooper, I think, was elected at the next election, which I suppose must have been in the spring of 1798, so that his congressional term commenced 4th of March, 1799, and expired with 3rd of March, 1801, when on the election of Mr. Jefferson, Judge Cooper, in a measure withdrew from active political life; though he remained a decided party man up to the time of his death. He was present at those ballottings in Congress, between Mr. Jefferson and Col. Burr, and with others of the Federal party, voted for the latter. He was so unwell at the time, that I believe he had to be carried into Congress to give his votes.

The 13th November, 1806, was the anniversary of my birth-day, when I became twenty-one years of age. Up to this time I had worked on the farm, the greater part of which was cleared and fenced; houses and barns had been erected; and a large orchard planted, which was fast coming to perfection. In the summer of 1805 or 1806, immediately after corn-planting, my father went to the northerly part of Wayne county, then nearly an unbroken wilderness. He went there with a view of selecting a larger quantity of land; and thus providing farms for myself and brothers. Our farm in Richfield, with its improvements, had become saleable and valuable; and would then have sold for as much if not more than at any subsequent period. Had he been suited with the country he went to explore, he intended to sell his farm and buy a tract of new land, large enough for several farms.

He crossed the Seneca, or Oswego river, at three-river point, and went to Williamson, in Wayne County. Fever and ague were so prevalent that he concluded not to purchase. The result of this exploration, I suppose, gave a cast to my subsequent pursuits for life. Had he purchased, I should undoubtedly have remained a farmer.

When he went away he directed me to cut and split rails and make a line fence through the woods, on the east line of the farm. The fence I was to make must have been from sixty to eighty rods long, which was nearly completed when he returned.

In the summer of 1842, before removing to Ohio, I had the curiosity to pass along through the woods, and see if any part of this fence remained; but there was not a vestige—neither log or rail remaining, of those I had split and placed there; nor was a single stump to be found of the trees I had cut down to make the fence. Everything had rotted away, and disappeared.

In the summer of 1805, I was in the meadow, mowing, when news arrived that Gen. Hamilton had fallen by Col. Burr.

In 1806, I was at work on the day of the great eclipse. I recollect precisely where and what I was doing; and the gloomy appearance at the time of total obscuration. The atmosphere became chilly. It appeared like the commencement of night: so much so that the fowls repaired to their roosts, as they do at night season. A more gloomy and at the same time grand spectacle could hardly be witnessed, than the coming on; the total eclipse; and then its passing off; till the sun appeared again, shorn of its beams, with all its strength and beauty.

The winter after I became of age, I kept school about four months; and so again the next winter; thus devoting myself, two winter seasons, to the humble but honorable avocation of country school keeping; boarding round among the proprietors. Not far from the time of closing my school, we got up a sleigh-ride and ball, and went to Winfield to hold it, about the 7th or 8th of April, 1807. A snow storm came on, which resulted in the greatest fall of snow I have ever known. The snow was so deep that it not only blocked up the roads, but covered the stumps and fences, so that there was no communication till the roads were partly shovelled and broken.

This snow remained during the greater part of the month, so that on election day of that year, which I think commenced the last Tuesday in April, it was very deep in the woods; but having thawed in the day, had, by freezing at night, formed a strong crust, on which I went to shoot partridges on their drumming logs in the morning.

At that election I gave my first vote, and voted the Democratic ticket. Daniel D. Tompkins, who was designated the "farmer's son," was our candidate for governor, and was elected over Morgan Lewis, who was up for re-election. The Federalists supported Gov. Lewis, with a portion of the Republicans; and these last were designated as "quids." Embargo times soon followed. Politics ran high. I was young, ardent, and active, and soon became a leader among the Democratic young men; and frequently acted as secretary of political meetings for the old. . . .

In the spring of 1808, I was elected constable, and again in 1809, in which capacity I served two years. This required my frequent attendance at Cooperstown, at court; and these attendances first suggested to me the propriety of turning my attention to the legal profession. I was not unaware of my defective education, and that it would be under discouraging auspices in case I attempted it. Reasoning on the subject, I satisfied myself that much might be done to overcome embarrassments by close application. From the time I became of age I had worked on the farm, at such times as I could spare, when not keeping school or engaged in my duties as constable. I consulted my father as to the propriety of entering a law office, and his advice was to follow the bent of my own inclinations.

Soon after, I went to Cherry Valley, and consulted with my friend Jabez D. Hammond, who was then in successful practice, with whom was associated James Brackett, as law partner. On informing them that I thought of entering upon legal studies, they both advised me to go-ahead, and kindly offered to enter my name as clerk in their office; lend me books till I got ready to go there permanently; and to impart such information as they could (classical and legal) whenever I should take my place in the office. This settled the question. In the fall of 1809, a certificate was filed of my clerkship; books were furnished which I took home with me, commencing with Blackstone's *Commentaries,* of course. These and other law books were read that year; and turning off all the business I could, as constable, I intended in the course of the coming winter, to review my English grammar, while my law studies were going on.

While acting as constable I had many adventures with those against whom I had warrants. On one occasion a fighting fellow, who had kept out of my way for some time, struck me violently on the head with a club, as I came suddenly on him in the morning. The blow stunned me slightly, but did not knock me down, as a stiff hat broke its force; he was soon mastered and marched off. Kind treatment on my part subdued him, so that from that time forward he always professed to be, and I think was, an ardent devoted friend. He seemed to like me the better for having ventured upon him armed as he was, after he had warned me to keep off.

I never found but one man, against whom I had process, who I hesitated to encounter, and he was a large stout-looking fellow, against whom I had an execution for a small military fine, which required me for want of property to take the body. He lived about ten miles from me, near the county line. On approaching him he sprang over the fence, seized a heavy stake, and stood at bay; declaring that he would not be taken and threatening to knock me down if I came over.

He had a sinister look that I did not like; pale, firm, and determined; his whole appearance indicated courage and desperation. Had he been charged with crime, I would have tried to take him; but for a paltry fine, when he might probably have to go to jail for the want of a few dollars, I thought it would be ridiculous to have my head broken, and had no desire to make the experiment. So, deeming "discretion the better part of valor," I rode off, and that was the last of it.

I was now preparing to leave Richfield, to pursue my legal studies in Cherry Valley; before going there I delivered a fourth of July oration, at Richfield in 1810, and in 1812 went from Cherry Valley to Winfield, Herkimer county, and delivered another on the fourth of July of that year.

FROM

Henry Clarke Wright's

Human Life

I

WHEN I was four years old, my father removed, with his family, into what was then called, in Connecticut, the Western country—now Central New York; and settled in the township of Hartwick, in the county of Otsego. I have an indistinct memory of parting with the old place and friends of that mountain home in Sharon—of the journey, in the depths of snow and a cold winter, with my mother and the younger children rolled up in blankets and over-coats, and stowed away in a sleigh—and of our arrival and settlement in our new home in the wilderness. For our home was surrounded by dark forests, only one family being settled within half a mile of us.

On our journey, we attempted to cross the Hudson river, at Albany, on the ice—about one quarter of a mile wide. The ice had become rotten, and water stood on the ice, as well as flowed under it. As the sleigh was crossing, in which were my mother and the younger children, one of the horses broke through the ice into the deep river. This caused great alarm, lest the whole should be dragged under and drowned. I remember the alarm and commo-tion, and the struggle to rescue the horse, and the success of it. Then my father turned back, and went six miles up the river to Troy, and crossed there.

Our new home was in a comparative wilderness. Not a house was in sight. The nearest neighbor on the south and east lived over a mile from us. On the west, the nearest lived three-fourths of a mile, and on the north, over one-fourth of a mile; and thick, dark forests intervened between us and them, except the one on the north. The farm which my father had bought contained 160 acres, and about half of it was cleared of the trees, though the stumps were for the most part remaining. The house was formed of wood, and covered with clapboards and shingles; and floored and ceiled inside with pine and hemlock boards. It stood close on the bank of a creek of clear, soft water, that served for all purposes of cooking, drinking and washing. To that babbling, bright brook, the children had to repair, morning and evening, to wash their hands, faces and feet. That brook, and an elm tree on its banks, near the house, under which I rolled, and romped, and shouted for joy of heart, are very dear objects of early recollection. A sawmill—invaluable items of living in a new country—was on this brook, a short way above our house, whose dam used, sometimes, to give way; and then, such a rush and roar of waters! sweeping fences, bridges, pigs, sheep and cattle away, and spreading wide the desolation. As a child, I used to think the geese were very silly creatures, in the coldest nights of winter, to sit in that brook all night, with their feet and legs in the water, and the ice all around them. I wondered at it. Many an hour, too, have I lain on the banks of that brook, and looked into its waters, and seen the cattle, bushes and trees, on the opposite bank, in the water, upside down. How the sun, moon, or stars, that I often saw in the bright water, came to be seen down there, was a marvel to me. When this mystery of a world beneath the water was first explained to me, it gave me infinite satisfaction.

Within twenty rods of the house, on the east, was a grove of huge pines, and beyond them lay the forest of nature, rising up the side of a mountain a mile high, close to the foot of which stood the house; so that the sun seldom shone upon us till about two hours after it had arisen. On the west, running north and south, was a mountain of about the same height, so that the sun went down to us long before its setting. My father's farm lay in the rich, narrow valley between the two mountains, extending up the sides of that on the east. The Otsego Creek [*sic.* actually Otego Creek] ran south under the base of the mountain on the west, and the bright and dearly remembered brook that ran by the door flowed into it. The large stream was called the "Great Creek," and the one by the house the "Small Creek." These mountains, on the east and west, were covered to their tops with native forest trees, of hemlock, pine, beech, birch, cherry, sugar maple, bird's-eye, curled maple, and other forest trees, of great height and circumference.

For many miles around us, most of the dwellings of the settlers, who had set down amid the forest, and made small clearings, or openings in it, were mere temporary houses of logs, laid one above the other; the ends, at the four corners, being notched to settle into one another, and the openings between the logs filled in with clay. The chimneys and hearths were made of stone, put together often without mortar, with huge fireplaces, in which logs and sticks of wood could be burnt from four to five feet long; and within these fireplaces often were stone seats, where persons could sit by the fire and gaze up out at the top of the chimney, and see the snow and rain come by day, or the stars twinkle by night. These log cabins cost from forty to fifty dollars each.

The floors of these primitive cabins were usually of boards, and altogether, they made comfortable dwellings, and could be divided into as many small rooms as were necessary. But the ambition of all settlers was to displace the log by a framed house, as soon as possible; but to do this, carpenters and house-joiners, and saw-mills and nails, were necessary, and these were not so easily obtained in new settlements. In building these framehouses, my father's services were in great demand. Many happy weeks and months have I spent in these log cabins, amid a surrounding wilderness, and felt secure from injury from man or beast, and that without lock or key, bolt or bar, police or military; and sounds that came up from that wilderness from ten thousand throats of insects, reptiles, beasts and birds, as the sun went down and night settled over the scene, were the sweet lullaby of my childhood.

My father lived ten miles from Cooperstown—so called, after the father of James Fenimore Cooper, the novelist. Judge Cooper, as he was called, at the close of the Revolutionary war, had come into possession of a vast tract of land in Otsego County, and had fixed his residence there, and in due time a village was formed. It was the county town, where lawyers and courts acted as the tools of the wrath and revenge of others, and where they dealt out what is called justice to their deluded clients. Never was a village more beautifully located. It stood at the south end or foot of Otsego Lake; a lake ten or twelve miles in length, and averaging from one and a half to two miles in breadth, and imbedded in mountains. From the south end of this lake issued the Susquehannah river, which, after winding its way many hundreds of miles to the south, through a rich and romantic valley, falls into the Chesapeake Bay. Cooperstown, though composed of few houses, and rude, with few exceptions, was the only market town for many miles around. Here the settlers went for articles of food and clothing which they could not raise and manufacture themselves. To my childish imagination, that rude, little village, with its few shops, was an object of deep interest; and when I first went with my father to that village, I could hardly conceive one more important and privileged than myself. It was an era in my life not to be forgotten; and no city, since seen, in America or Europe, has effaced the impression then received; and to this day, I regard that then little village of cabins, (now a large town,) on the shore of Otsego Lake, and surrounded with forest on all sides but one (the Lake) with a feeling of awe and interest which I attach to no other city or town.

The death of my mother was an event that deeply affected the happiness of the family, and the first to give me an idea of death as applying to human beings. I was five years old. It was evening. My father had just come home from his labor abroad. We were all seated around the supper table. The scene is fresh in my mind. One of my sisters anxiously cried out, "Mother, what is the matter?" She answered, sweetly and calmly, "Don't be alarmed about me; all is well." This called the attention of my father and all to her. She was carried to her bed, and never spoke again. In a few hours she was dead. She died of apoplexy. I stood by her bedside, frightened to see her so pale, silent and motionless. My heart was heavy, for I was told that she would never look at me nor speak to me again. The neighbors came in for miles around. They took away my mother, to bury her in the ground, as I was told. All the family went away with her, except myself and a younger brother, who were left in charge of a kind neighbor. I looked out of the window, and saw them carry her away. My young heart was desolate when I found my mother was no more to come back. But I brooded over my feelings in silence. Only into the bosom of an older sister, who became to me as a mother, could I pour my aching heart. She talked to me of my mother, and called out my sympathies. . . . My mother was buried at the foot of a high hill, or cliff, amidst some beech and pine trees, in a solitary spot, which, in after life, was often visited by me.

To my young heart, my father's house ceased to be a home when my mother was carried out of it, no more to return. I heard my father speak and read of the dead being raised up, and this made me hope that my mother might be raised and brought home; for I could have no idea of death, except the body becoming cold and silent, and being buried in the ground. I felt a longing in my heart, for a time, that nothing could fill; a sense of loneliness which no kindness could cheer. . . .

After some months, my father married again, and brought another woman into the house, whom I was told to call mother; but it was long before I could call her so. It seemed to me a falsehood, for I knew that she was a stranger, not my mother. She took charge of the younger children, four of us, all boys.

My step-mother bore three children, daughters, to my father, of whom I was very fond. I had no greater enjoyment than attending to them, in carrying them in my arms, playing with them, and making them happy. I would have left any sports to care for those sisters; and when I came from school, or was freed from other labors, I would go to the house to be with them. When they were sick, I felt an indescribable anxiety and desolation, and could neither eat nor sleep, play nor work, in any comfort, and only wished to linger around their cradle, to rock them, to be near and to watch them.

About two years after my mother died, my brother, whose name was Milton, and who, being about two years older than myself, was my most intimate playmate in the family, followed her to the grave. This was a great loss to me; for he was a bold, generous, active boy, and my spirit chimed in with his more than with any other member of the family. I loved his reckless daring, and restless activity. He was seized with a nervous or brain fever, and, in a few days, was dead.

I have a vivid recollection of his death. It was midnight; I was in my bed, and, with the rest of the family, was called up to be present at the closing scene. I came down in haste; entered the room; my dying brother and playfellow was sitting in a chair. All the family were standing around. I stood near my brother. He spoke not a word—did not seem to see or know any of us. That room was silent, disturbed only by the short breathings of my dying brother, and the stifled sobs of the loving ones around him. How I longed to hear that brother's voice speaking to me! But he ceased to breathe, and was laid on the bed. Then came the funeral, of which I remember only the neighbors coming in, and the last look at my playmate and bedfellow brother, as he lay in his coffin. He looked so pale, and seemed so still and silent! I could not understand it. What mystery is in death, to young children! . . . I was told that God had killed him. I could not understand it. My feelings were dark and unreconciled. I heard my father and others speak of God as loving and kind to all, but how could he be so and kill my brother, and take him from all his sports, in which he so delighted, I could not understand. I was seven years old, and I had many such thoughts about my brother's death. These perplexities were in me; I could not avoid them; and if I had had some one to speak to me affectionately and cheerfully, to bring them out and explain them, it would have given me relief, and spared me many sad hours, then and afterward.

I am persuaded the practice of investing death with terror and gloom, by parents, teachers, and clergymen, is dishonorable to Him who has wisely and lovingly appointed man to die, and is attended with pernicious consequences. Natural death is not a natural calamity, but is as really the fruit of divine love and goodness as are life and health. As well characterize the change of a caterpillar from the chrysalis to the butterfly state as a natural evil. The death of the body, so far from being a punishment for sin, is designed to be a most joyous and longed-for change of the mode of existence—an introduction to a higher, more happy, and more beautiful state of being. It should be presented to children as an angel of love and beauty, and not as an insatiable monster, existing only to devour.

But my brother was carried away from me, and laid beside my mother at the foot of the hill under the beech trees. I was taken along with the rest to see it done. It was done by the neighbors, and we all stood round looking on, till they had put him in the ground and covered him up; and then my father, according to custom, took off his hat, and thanked them for their kindness to him, in his sorrow, in helping him to bury his dead. We all went home, and I went to the places where my brother and I had played together, and then I felt most deeply my bereavement. I gathered together his little playthings, and kept them long as mementos of my departed playmate. In time, the sorrow and loneliness caused by his death passed from my mind; but the effects of that event have never ceased. . . .

From the age of six or seven, my recollection of the employments and leading events of my childhood is vivid and distinct. I will proceed to relate some of them as they occur to me. I include the first twelve years of my life as the period of my childhood.

A desire to know how to do and to do, whatever I saw others do, is one of my earliest remembered impressions; and, fortunately, my father and mother, and brothers and sisters, never checked that desire, but encouraged it, and gave me abundant opportunity to gratify it. As a child, I felt that I could learn to do any thing, whether it required bodily or mental effort, which I saw others do. I had unbounded confidence in myself, and laughed at difficulties. My spirit was buoyant, confident, restless and impatient under restraints, not self-imposed. I did feel as a child, and have always felt since, though of course I could not give expression of the feeling then as I can now, that I was competent to be a church, a priesthood, a government, an empire, in myself, and I never could see good reason why any created being should exercise authority over me. This feeling may be natural to all children. It was certainly deep and strong in me, and had it been encouraged and properly directed, I had been spared many bitter mental conflicts in after life.

The five youngest of my father's children by his first wife were sons, and my own sisters were women grown; the eldest being married, and away to a home of her own; the other two were about to marry. Of course, my step-mother was mainly destitute of female help in the cares of the family except what was hired; consequently, much of the in-door labor fell upon the younger boys. I have alluded to my employment as care-taker of my sisters, and my delight therein. I record, with satisfaction, the fact that I learned to cook. Many an Indian meal pudding and Johnnycake have I made, and many a dish of fried ham and eggs have I prepared. Many a dish of "potluck" (as boiled salt beef and pork and vegetables were called) have I prepared, and served up to my father and brothers for dinner; many a dish of tea have I made for others, though I never drank many myself; many a dish of hash have I prepared and warmed, and served up for breakfast; many times have I set the table, cleared it away, washed, wiped, and set up the dishes; many times have swept the floor, made the beds, pounded the clothes in washing, wrung them, and hung them out to dry; and at all these matters I was counted handy, and am thankful I was put to do these things, for these little every day matters help to make up life. And truly can I say, I felt a pride and pleasure in doing them, and in feeling that the responsibility was cast upon me, knowing that I was contributing to the support and comfort of my parents and brothers and sisters.

The clothing of the family, whether of linen or wool, was spun and woven in the house. I never spun or wove, but for many a piece of cloth have I spooled the warp and quilled the wool. But this employment of spooling and quilling, I never liked—it required too little action. I was abundantly indoctrinated into the mysteries of chopping and splitting wood—of picking up chips, getting kindling wood, making fires. In all these household employments, so necessary to the cleanliness, comfort and existence of the family, I took real pride and pleasure; and I love to record the fact, for I wish to be of no reputation among those low, miserable creatures, who deem these necessary labors unpleasant and degrading. I had not the least suspicion that I was doing anything mean and servile, or at all derogatory to the dignity of my nature. The thought never entered my mind, then, that, as a son, or a brother, I was out of my sphere; nor have I been able, since, to see that I was. When doing work; when preparing food for my little sisters, and feeding them, carrying them about in my arms, and singing them to sleep, or romping and rolling about the grass or floor with them, giving up my whole soul to their comfort and amusement, or when engaged in these household labors, had any boy, or man, laughed, or pointed the finger at me, and tried to make game of me, as one engaged in doing what was mean and unbecoming; I believe, child as I was, an innate sense of their meanness and injustice, and a feeling that I was doing what was contributing to the comfort and support of my parents and brothers and sisters, would have saved me from any feeling of shame. I do not remember that the least sense of impropriety, or of unwillingness to be seen by any body in doing these things, ever entered my heart. Certain I am, that I used to feel unmixed satisfaction, and a conscious sense of dignity and importance when my step-mother used to confide to my care my little sisters in a protracted ramble in the pastures, meadows and woods, to pick berries or gather flowers; or when she put me to do any work that contributed to the comfort and necessities of the family. . . .

My labors, as a child, were not confined to the house. To saddle and ride, to harness and drive, horses; to yoke and drive oxen; to fodder the cattle, and do all work about the barn, were the accomplishments and the special objects of the ambition of my childhood. It was a work of special desire to me to learn to milk the cows, and when I did learn, I had enough of it. At eight years of age, I was an adept in this art. I never knew what fear of horses or horned cattle was. I always felt that I could control them, and I did, whenever I had the care of them. One circumstance in regard to a cow was a mystery to me then, and has been ever since. It is this:

When about ten years old, my father had a cow of his own raising. A beautiful, finely-formed beast she was, with white feet and face, and wild, restless, fiery eyes. I had to milk her, and it was long before I could subdue that wild creature so that she would quietly let me do it. It was mainly with her heels that she used to do mischief. Many a time has she kicked me over and my milk, drenching me with it from head to foot, and then ran, clearing fences and bars, and distancing all pursuit. But she never escaped me. I always brought her back, and gained my point in controlling her. My conflicts with that cow became a source of exciting pleasure to me, though they cost me many weary runs and perilous struggles, for sometimes she came at me with her horns as well as her heels.

The pleasure and pride of my heart, in gaining a triumph over that wild beast, and the meekness and docility with which she always yielded in the end, fully compensated for all the toil. I named her Nimbleshanks, for her fleetness, and her agility in leaping over fences. Often she would come to me, and put herself in a posture for milking; but this only in her pleasantest moods. Often, of her own accord, she would go into the corner where I kept the whip, as if conscious of being in a mood to need its restraining influence. There was certainly a strange sympathy between me and that wild, reckless creature; and I used to think she had reason, as well as instinct, to direct, for she certainly understood me far better than some of my human playmates. The following is a fact in regard to that animal:

She had kicked me and my milk over one evening, splashing the milk all over me. I drove her into a corner, and began to whip her. There was no way of escaping the storm of blows which I showered upon her. All at once, she dropped upon her knees; and there she was, standing on her feet behind, and resting on her knees before, and her head bent round to me, as it seemed to me, with an expression of sadness and gentleness in her eyes, such as I never saw before. I stopped whipping, in amazement, and was deeply moved to see that subdued expression of suffering. I laid aside the whip, and from that hour, whenever I went to whip her for her kickings, she would drop on her knees, and there remain till I had done the milking. I could not whip her while she was in that position. The strange conduct of that cow was a subject of great wonderment. Old Nimbleshanks, as she came to be generally called, was counted a knowing one. Many a pailful of flowing milk have I taken from her, and treated myself to many drinks of it as I was milking; for I preferred hers to that of any of the others.

Driving the cows to and from their pasture, morning and evening, was, for several years, a stated part of my labor. As was, also, the care of the sheep, which were left to wander about and pick a living in the woods—the leader of the flock usually wearing a little bell, suspended by a leather thong around his neck. The music of these bells, suspended around the necks of sheep and cattle as they fed in the woods, was very sweet to me. Many times have I skimmed over the pastures, barefooted, on frosty mornings; stopping at every stone big enough to plant a foot upon, and then balancing myself, first on one foot and then on the other, to warm my feet, the stone having more heat than the frosty grass. It was my delight to hunt after the sheep in the woods, to run under dark tree-tops, and whistle, sing, and shout, and listen to the echoes of my own merry voice and song in the forest. I was then, and am now, fond of all domestic fowls and animals; and it has been good for me that I had much to do with them as a child.

I had an ambition, as all children brought up on farms have, to ride and manage horses; and according to the opinion of my eldest brother, I attained to great tact in the equestrian art. At any rate, he made me ride horse for him to plough many an acre, and under many scorching suns. This kind of riding—slowly moving round and round in a field, under a broiling sun, and day after day, and all day—was not to my liking. I used to go asleep, and be in danger of falling headlong, and incurring the sharp rebukes of my brother by letting the horses go wrong.

In no one thing did I more desire to perfect myself than in the art of mowing and reaping. To use a scythe and sickle well was accounted a necessary accomplishment. And these I did learn, thoroughly; and in the work of haying and harvesting, I ever took delight; not as a looker-on of other people's labors, but a workman myself with the scythe, the sickle, and the pitchfork. The smell of new-made hay is more delicious to me than that of the choicest perfumery; and the sight of mowers mowing down a meadow in the dewy morn, and of children tossing the grass to dry, and of reapers reaping down the harvest-fields, is more picturesque and pleasant than the sight of a gala on the coronation day of kings and queens. I love those rural scenes. I know what they are, and have been a part of them; and I had rather be a part of them again, than of the pageantry of the proudest aristocracy and royalty on earth. I had rather know how to till the earth, to mow and reap, than to be an adept in all the games and amusement ever invented by the wealthy or the worthless to kill time. I am thankful for the desire to work, and for having been habituated, in childhood, to feed and clothe myself by the labor of my own hands. . . .

Among other labors which I learned to perform, was that of making sugar from the sap of the sugar maple. This is a tall, beautiful tree, and is coming to be used very generally in Ohio, Pennsylvania, New York, and the New England States, as an ornamental tree. It was known to me in childhood by the name of hard maple, to distinguish it from another species, called the soft maple. The latter is full of sap, but it is of no use. From the former, my father made all of his sugar and molasses. Till I was fifteen years old, I never tasted any other.

The first opening of spring is the only time to make it, as the sap of the tree begins to circulate, and the buds begin to swell. A place is selected in the woods where a sufficient number of trees grow within convenient distances of one another. Small spouts are prepared to conduct the sap from the tree, and little troughs or buckets are made to receive it. As many trees are tapped as are needed, and each tree produces from two to three pounds of sugar. The sap is carried, in pails, to some central place, and there turned into kettles, or cauldrons, and boiled down to a syrup. The process of boiling down is carried on night and day in the woods, during the short period of the running of the sap, which seldom extends over three or four weeks. A little shed or shanty is built near the place of boiling, into which the children and persons attending the sugar-making can enter to rest by day or night. The sap is boiled down, so that many pailsful are comprised in one, and this syrup is carried to the house, and there further purified and reduced to sugar.

The sugar camp—as the place is called—is an object of great attraction to all the junior branches of the family. It was so to me; not only because there I could drink of the syrup, and make candy, but because of the kind of life which is there lived. It is a time of intense excitement to the whole family. Those who spend the night in the woods are excited by the scenery and the circumstances; and those who are at home, in beds, are excited on account of the loved ones who are out in the forest. Often have I, when a child, wandered alone into the forest to the sugar camp, to carry food to those who were there employed; and in doing so, I felt great enjoyment. I was proud of the trust, and exulted when I trod the ground under the giant forest trees, or pushed my way through dark and almost impenetrable thickets.

I loved to wander in the woods alone, by day or night. To see and feel the gathering gloom of night settling around me; to feel myself shrouded in forest darkness, far from the footsteps of man, with a dog, seemed to me the consummation of earthly felicity. In the sugar camp, or "sugar bush," I used, as a child, to enjoy this feeling of deep solitude, of stern desolation, and proud independence, which comes over the mind when surrounded by a thick and extensive forest—especially if the time were evening, and the forest were of dark evergreen. It seemed to me a great boon, to be allowed to spend the night with my father or elder brothers in the sugar bush. There have I sat many an hour by a huge fire, whose brightness shone upon the bushes and trees near by, only to make the darkness more intense and appalling. There, by that fire, have I sat and looked off into the impenetrable gloom; thinking of the wild beasts or wild Indians that lived in those forest solitudes. Every now and then the fire must be replenished, and more sap poured into the kettles. Then to go into the shanty, and lie down on straw, or dried leaves, and there lie and look out upon the flickering, tremulous light which the fire reflected on the trunks and branches of the trees, and to look up through those lofty tree-tops at the moon or stars, that appeared so sparkling and beautiful in the vaulted sky; it was most instructive to me.

I was a child—my thoughts and feelings were those of a child; but then and there I received impressions of God, and of my self, and my destiny, more cheerful, more purifying, ennobling, and life-like, than I ever received in a meeting-house, or theological seminary, or from catechisms or ministers. My young heart felt that the woods, the winds that moaned through their tops, the darkness, the blue sky, the moon and stars, were the work of an unseen Hand, and it made me feel happy to think of that unseen though not unfelt Being who made what I saw then. I used to feel that my mother and my brother were with Him, and that I should like to be with Him too. That Being, as I thought of Him, by night, in the sugar bush, seemed very loveable and near to me, far more so than he did in the theology and religion which I was taught; for, as He appeared in these, I could not love Him, nor could I wish to see Him or go near Him.

I was an earnest, joyous child, as intent, for the time being, in whatever sports I undertook, as I was in other useful employments. Earnest playing was as necessary to my well-being, mentally, morally, and physically, as earnest labor. But I had no enjoyment in sports that required little or no bodily activity. I never learned to play marbles, backgammon, dice, or cards. To this day, I am as ignorant of these games as I was at my birth. Playing ball was a favorite pastime; as were running, hopping and leaping. I was fond of climbing trees, hanging by my hands or by my feet on the limbs, dangling in the air. I never could endure fishing. To sit for hours holding a hook in the water, to lure fish to their death under pretence of kindness, was a sport for which I had not the least inclination; and though a brook ran close to the door, full of trout, that I saw sporting in their element every day, I never hooked two dozen fish from the water in my life. Nor did I ever aspire to shoot birds or beasts. I used to delight in handling the bow and arrow, though with these I never had much pleasure in killing any thing—not because I felt it to be wrong (as I do now believe it wrong to destroy animal life for amusement), but simply because I took no pleasure in it.

There was one source of enjoyment which exerted a powerful influence over me. I was excessively fond of hearing old people tell stories about Indian wars and massacres, and about ghosts and witches. The Indians had not then disappeared from those regions, and a belief in ghosts and witches was then very general.

A very old woman, known among the children as Aunt Huldah, lived half a mile from my father's, in a low log hut. Many winter and autumn evenings have I sat in the corner of Aunt Huldah's fireplace, and, with other children, listened to her stories. She had many about Indian wars, about desperate encounters of men with bears, and panthers, and wolves; but she excelled in telling stories about witches and ghosts. She was a firm believer in these beings, and had often seen them herself—as she believed.

She was somewhat palsied; but she loved the children, and they loved her. That kind, and, as the children believed, eloquent old woman, and the scene around her fire, still live brightly in my memory. There she sat, in a low chair, with her elbows resting on her knees, and her chin resting on her two hands, her head shaking from palsy, and looking into a huge, blazing fire of wood, which lighted up the low room dimly. There was no candle or lamp; a group of young children hovered around the fire and Aunt Huldah, all clamorous for a story; the rain pattering, the storm howling, or the moon or stars glistening without, as the case might be. Aunt Huldah would begin her story about the adventures of a witch or ghost, and grow warmer, more animated, and more eloquent, as she proceeded. Her eyes would become distended and wild looking, and her head would shake more rapidly; and our eyes stared, and our mouths gaped, and our breath stopped, in wonder and sympathy. Often have I been so wrought up by that old woman's eloquent stories, that my heart seemed to stand still, and my eyes to glare like balls of fire. I dared not breathe, or look behind me to the door or window, or up the chimney, or into the fire, or into a distant and dark corner of the room, for fear of seeing some of the terrible beings that she was describing. I could look no where but straight into Aunt Huldah's face and eyes, and even there I seemed to see all the scenes and creatures of which she was speaking. . . .

Many ghosts were seen in that region, and many witches and wizards worked wonders there during my childhood. It was a new country; the population was scattered, living mostly in log-houses, with small clearings; around them were deep forests, filled with wild beasts and Indians, from which came up strange and unearthly sounds.

A deep, impenetrable swamp, filled with hemlock trees

and bushes, commenced near my father's house and extended a mile south and west. It was a narrow, deep ravine, and a road ran along on the brow of the steep hill that led down to it. That seemed to me, as a child, the embodiment of all that was gloomy and appalling. When eight or nine years old, I have rode through those woods, on the margin of that terrible ravine, in darkness in which eyes were useless, and listened with stern delight to the voices that came up from it. In the spring and summer, as the sun went down, the frogs, toads, lizards, serpents, owls, foxes, wolves, and millions of insects that burrowed in that swamp, held their grand concerts. In the gathering gloom, I have sat on the fence, by the spring, or brook, on the door step, or under the trees, and listened with rapture to that wild forest music. It generally lasted till nine or ten, and then the whippoorwill, with its plaintive solo, would close the concert, and say good night. Nothing connected with my childhood affects me so wildly, so sweetly, so soothingly, as this.

Such a region was the fit place for supernatural agents to come and work their pleasure. Ghosts appeared there, to reveal some appalling murder, some hidden treasure, or to give warning of some death or some approaching calamity; and witches came to pinch and prick the bodies of men and women, to put on them the witch's bridle, turn them into horses in a twinkling, and ride them madly through the country, to some gathering of witches and devils; or to fly through the neighborhood, and over the tops of the forests, on broomsticks; to creep into an enemy's house in the shape of a black cat, with peering eyes of fire; to destroy the poultry, the pigs, and to set the cattle running wild and mad; or to blight the corn, sour the milk or cream, and thus gratify revenge, and resent deeply cherished insults and injuries. Many times, when a child, have I heard men and women speak of these things as having been seen and experienced by themselves. I thought that it was wrong to doubt the existence, the appearance, and the agency of ghosts and witches, because the Bible said, "suffer not a witch to live," and because of the Witch of Endor. . . .

Stories of Indian tortures and burnings; of Indian tomahawks, and scalping-knives; stories of encounters with wild beasts, of dark nights spent in the woods, and of hairbreadth escapes from the wild dangers of wading and swimming rivers, and crossing mountain torrents; stories of children strayed or lost, or torn to pieces, or starved to death in the woods; these, and the like stories, relating to the actual, living world around us, were very different matters. Ghosts and witches might horrify and astound the neighborhood, but they never made vacant the place of some loved one at the table, and around the domestic fireside. They made the hair stand on end, but they never made the heart sad. . . .

My father had a fierce, wild, reckless dog. There was nothing he would not encounter at the word of command, and in defence of the children whose protection he considered as his peculiar province. To climb hills and rocks, with that dog; to push my way through swamps and thickets; to tree squirrels and partridges, and there leave them; to climb into tops of bushes and trees, and there sit for hours, used to fill my cravings equal to any other pleasure.

Sliding down steep hills on the frozen snow, on a hand sled, was a favorite amusement in winter. Many hundreds of times have I toiled to get my little sled and myself to the top of some steep hill, solely to enjoy the pleasurable excitement of darting down again, like an arrow. I used to think hills were made chiefly for boys to slide down. But in pursuing this sport, I have had many rollings in the snow.

One of the richest and sweetest sources of my enjoyment, as a child, was found in the company of my little sisters. Their laughter and their tears were mine. To wander about the fields with them; to pick berries and weave nosegays for them, and make them happy, was my delight. They seemed soft and gentle to me, and this part of my nature was filled in their company; while the opposite extreme of my nature, *i.e.*, daring hardihood, restless energy, and unbending determination, was fully gratified by bolder and more active sports.

As I look back, I can easily see that those amusements which brought me least into competition for mastery with others did me most good. I am very certain that every sport that led me to contend for mastery over my playmates always did me harm, engendering a spirit at war with that of self-forgetfulness and self-sacrifice. As I have tried to cultivate the spirit that would lead me to suffer rather than make others suffer, and to die, rather than be a cause of death to others, many of the sports of my childhood have exerted a powerful influence against me. Wrestling, running and jumping, playing ball, and the like— games of which I was extremely fond, and which, as I played them brought me into direct competition with others for the mastery—were all hurtful to my spirit, however they may have tended to give strength and health to my body. He or she would be one of mankind's greatest benefactors, who would invent some vigorous, active, healthful sports for children, which would not bring them into an exciting competition for mastery over one another, and which, instead of selfishness, would be promotive of benevolence.

My first recollections of a school-house are of an old log building, rudely put together; a huge fireplace, with a mighty chimney of stones, loosely piled together; a floor of boards, rough, and not nailed down; and standing on the bank of a rapid brook, not a stone's throw from a grove of huge hemlock trees; the very location being enough to frighten young children, not familiar with such things, out of their wits. To get to this desolate house, that might well be said to be haunted, I had to pass through a wood of unusual loneliness about one mile; but when I reached the school, I had my sister for my first teacher.

An incident is remembered touching that school, that afforded no little amusement to teacher and children. One day, a large black snake thrust his head up through a hole in the floor, and drew his body up two or three feet, and there he lay, calmly and leisurely looking about him, as if contemplating the teacher and children to see whether he should join us. There was great fun about the black snake coming to school, and inquiries made of him by the children, as to what he wished to learn, and to whom should be given the honor of teaching his snakeship his letters. He lay there some time, looking very meek and quiet, though when exicited, that species of the serpent has an eye that gleams with great fierceness, though not with the deadly malignity of the rattlesnake. The black snake's bite is harmless; he injures only by getting the victim into his powerful coil. Neither the teacher nor the children had any fear of their visitor. He was allowed to stay as long as he pleased, and then to retire unmolested. After this, we had a visit from him frequently. He would thrust his head out first and look about, then draw his body out and coil himself up on the floor, and there he would seem to look and listen, with great satisfaction, to the hum and buzz of the school. That snake became an object of interest and sympathy to the whole school; we had no more thought of disturbing or injuring it than we had of injuring one another. We called him the learned snake, because he came to school; and he probably got about as much learning as some of the rest of us.

I remember, too, the stupid process of learning the alphabet, and to put letters into syllables, and syllables into words, and words into sentences. I could not then understand the difficulty, but I know it was a practice calculated to disgust children with all books and book learning. The children that were learning the alphabet were called up, two or three at a time; the teacher held the book before them, and pointed with a knife to the first letter and said A. Then the children repeated A after her. Then she pointed to B, and told the children to say B, and they said B, with their eyes, perhaps, fixed on the floor, or turned askance at some other scholar, or half asleep. So the process went on to the last letter. Then the children sat down, and there we had to sit, with nothing to do; no pictures to look at, no slates and pencils to draw the figures of letters, nothing in the world to rouse stupidity or instruct ignorance; and not a single familiar object or thing associated with the letters, syllables and words that we had to say over. In this way, I was thoroughly drilled into the art of saying over letters, syllables and words, and spelling them, without exciting one emotion, or one thought of persons and things as they existed around me. No wonder we all broke forth from such a place at recess, and when school was dismissed, with an irrepressible shout of joy at our momentary deliverance. It has often been a doubt in my mind, if my school and book learning during my childhood did me more good than harm. I know it did me great harm; I do not know that it did me much good.

During the period of my childhood—from about five to twelve years of age—I was kept at school, on an average, about eight months per year; about five months in summer, under female teachers, and the other months in winter, always under male teachers. In spite of the disgusting and untoward circumstances attending the schools and manner of teaching, I became fond of going to school and of study; though the study did little else for me but to exercise and strengthen my memory. It did nothing to teach me how to think, to reflect on what I felt within me, or saw or heard around me; nothing to rouse, invigorate, and discipline my affections or my intellect. . . .

I did indeed learn to spell, to read and write my native language, and also to know common Arithmetic—and this was important; but no Geography, no Grammar, no History, no Anatomy, no Physiology, no Astronomy, was taught there. These I acquired by myself, during intervals and hours of relaxation from other pursuits in after life. For whatever development and discipline my intellectual or moral powers ever had, I certainly am not much indebted to the lessons of the schoolmaster, or to the prayers and sermons of priests. Their influence, so far as they had any, was rather to crush and palsy the intellect, to blight and wither the heart, by stifling inquiry, and circumscribing the affections to the narrow dimensions of a sect or a nation.

The first time there was oral stated prayer, in a school that I attended, it had a most pernicious effect upon my mind. The master was a preacher, very moving in prayer, earnest in exhortation, and terrible in his rebukes to sinners. He was a famous man, was that Elder, in strengthening the stakes and lengthening the cords of his sect.

The school house was a small building, and the children were all within the length of his arm and his rod. He was a fiery tempered man, and as unfit to have the management of children, as a wolf to have the guardianship of lambs. He was a hard drinker of whiskey. Every day he had his bottle of whiskey in a little closet behind his desk, and the key of which he carried in his pocket. Often, during the school hours, did that bad man slip into his closet to take his dram. He used to send the older boys to a whiskey shop, near by, for his liquor. He seldom closed his school at evening by saying prayers, except in a state of intoxication. He always grew savage as he grew more drunken; and the children were sure to feel his heavy rod, towards evening, without mercy. His anxiety to have us converted was in proportion to the degree of his drunkenness. When he became especially drunk, he was especially concerned for our souls—but then he had no mercy on our bodies; and many times have I seen him sitting in his chair in the middle of the room, with that long whip in his hand, giving the children a most tender exhortation, and telling us how he loved our souls—the tears streaming down the while; and if there was a smile of scorn or of ridicule on the part of any child, old or young, down came the whip upon him or her with a will. It became a byeword with the children, "prayers for the soul, and whips for the body." . . .

He always stood up in the middle of the room—holding on by his chair. He was a strong built man—had a broad flat face, short neck, piercing black small eyes, sunk far into his head, peering out venomously from under huge, overhanging eyebrows. He wore spectacles, but in saying prayers turned them up on to the top of his head. He would slowly and solemnly rise up from his chair, and in a stern voice call out to the children, "Arise!" We would jump to our feet. Then he would call out "Attend!" At which we would fold our hands before us, and turn our eyes down upon the floor and look devout. Then he would survey us for a moment, and begin to say his prayers.

The image of that horrid man will ever haunt my mind. There he stood in the centre of the floor; his long whip, with which he could reach to every corner of the room, brandished in his right hand, holding on to the back of the chair with his left; his spectacles resting on the top of his bald head; his fierce and fiery eyes peering out from under his shaggy eye-brows upon the children; for he always said prayers with his eyes open. He began to say his prayers; and he would go on telling God what depraved little creatures we were; how we were more inclined to be unkind than kind, to be cruel than gentle, to hate than to love, and to injure than to do good to one another—for he always told the Lord about this, in saying his evening prayers; and as he would ask God to give us new hearts, his glowering, fierce eyes were watching the children, and if one happened to look round to another, or to move, or to smile, or to assume a look and make a motion that he thought not devotional, down came the long whip upon our shoulders and backs, and he would be saying his prayer to God at the same time, asking Him to have mercy on our depraved souls. Sometimes he would stop his prayer, and accompany his blows with some objurgatory epithets, calling out to us, "Be serious, Mary," "Be prayerful, John," "Look devout, Henry." Then he would go on saying his prayer. Such is a true picture of that man's saying prayers in his school. The effect on my mind was to disgust me with the name of prayer. . . . But the drunken Elder was dismissed after about two months. Our bodies were rescued from his blows; our souls from his prayers.

In all the schools I attended during my childhood, it was customary to stimulate children to study by arranging them in competition one against another. To quicken the competition, tickets were given to him or her who happened to be at the head of the class. Prizes were promised to the person in the class who, at the end of the school, had the most tickets. In the summer, when I was eight years old, two prizes were offered; one, a book to be given to the child in the first class in spelling, who should have the most tickets when the term was half done; the other, a penknife, to be given to the child who, at the close of the term, had the most tickets. For the first prize I worked hard, and obtained it. What was it? A pictorial story of Bluebeard. I had heard Aunt Huldah relate that horrible story, without any abatement of its horribleness. I longed for it, and was determined to get it; and I did. I devoured it with frightful eagerness. That story, with the horrid colored pictures, powerfully affected my mind; and I kept the book for many years. Then came the hot competition for the other prize—the penknife—and a beautiful little one it was. I was resolved to have that, too; but in addition to getting the most tickets, another task was to be accomplished; *i.e.*, learning to repeat a little poem, entitled the "Bird's Nest." The following is the sweet poem:

> Yes, little nest, I'll hold you fast,
>   And little birds—one, two, three, four;
> I've watched you long, you're mine at last—
>   Poor little things, you'll 'scape no more.
>
> Chirp, cry, and flutter, as you will,
>   Ah! simple rebels! 'tis in vain;
> Your little wings are unfledged still,
>   How can you freedom, then, obtain?
>
> What note of sorrow strikes my ear?
>   Is it their mother thus distressed?
> Ah, yes! and see, their father dear
>   Flies round and round, to seek their nest.
>
> And is it I who cause their moan?
>   I, who so oft in summer's heat,
> Beneath yon oak have laid me down,
>   To listen to their songs so sweet.

If from my tender mother's side,
    Some wicked wretch should make me fly,
Full well I know 'twould her betide,
    To break her heart, to sink, to die.

And shall I then so cruel prove,
    Your little ones to force away?
No, no! together live and love;
    See, here they are! take them, I pray.

Teach them in yonder wood to fly,
    And let them your sweet warbling hear;
Till their own wings can soar as high,
    And their own notes may sound as clear.

Go, gentle birds! go, free as air;
    While oft again, in summer's heat,
To yonder oak I will repair,
    And listen to your songs so sweet.

I learned that little poem, and it powerfully wrought upon me respecting robbing birds' nests—a thing which I had never done before. I obtained the second prize, though it gave me little pleasure to take it. The child that had the next highest number of tickets was a bright, sweet-tempered little girl, of my own age. She obtained as many tickets as I did, save one, and learned the poem as perfectly as I did. During nearly the whole term, we sat together in the class. We were generally together during play hours, and often, when not at school, she was my playfellow. She loved me, and I loved her, as children love, purely and tenderly. I obtained the prize, and she was sad. I would have given it to her, but the teacher interfered to prevent me. I felt very sorrowful, as I saw the sadness of my playmate. I took no comfort in that knife. I went home with it, and started off to the pasture to drive home the cows; and was whittling a bit of stick, and cut one of my fingers about half off. This settled the affair of the knife; I gave it to my next older brother, for some trifle of no value.

I have said I was the tenth of my father's eleven children by his first wife. The eleventh was a boy some two and a half years younger than myself. During the summer in which I obtained the prizes, I was allowed to take this younger brother with me to school. This I counted a favor, as he was company for me, going and returning; and a bright, active little fellow he was, though not as strong and hardy as myself. He was quick to anger, and as quickly over it. This being my brother's first essay at schooling, he did not know how to act, and of course said and did all sorts of out-of-the-way things. He often outraged school proprieties by speaking aloud whatever he happened to think, and by running about the room as he liked. Many a contest did he have with the teacher, before he could be drilled into the business of sitting still and silent, with his hands folded in his lap, for hours at a time. Poor little fellow! I used to feel for him, and wish I could take the brunt of his trials and labors upon myself; but I could no nothing for him. At length he was brought under the standing orders of the school; but the process of subduing had well-nigh sickened him of the school for ever. I used to initiate the little fellow into the mysteries of climbing trees, clambering over and through fences, jumping over and wading through brooks, walking on the top rail of fences, standing on the head, walking on the hands, and throwing the heels over the head, touching only the hand to the ground; while the teacher initiated him into the mysteries of sitting still and silent with folded hands, and of saying his letters. I think he profited most by my instructions. But on one occasion, my teaching had well-nigh cost him his life.

The time was harvest. We came home from school. I took my brother into the barn. My step-mother and a young hired girl were in the house; my brothers were in a distant field reaping; my father was from home. We entered the barn, and I closed the door, thinking that we would get upon the new-mown hay there, and have a fine time tumbling about and leaping from the beams, throwing our bodies over and over before we struck the hay. But a large cart, with two wheels, was on the barn floor, with a load of wheat sheaves on it. The pole of the cart rested on a block of wood, so high that the whole body and load of the cart rather inclined backward; so that a little increase of weight behind would drag body, load and all, down behind. As I passed the back end of the cart, I sprang up and caught hold of a high round of the ladder—as the rick was called that constituted the hindmost end of the cart body—to have a swing, and called to my brother to catch hold of a round lower down, and we would have a fine time together. He did so; and, in a moment, up flew the fore end of the cart, tongue, load and all, and turned over upon us. There we both were, flat on our backs; the rounds of the ladder lying across our breasts and stomachs, and the whole load pressing upon us. At that moment, I thought not of myself; my concern was for my brother, whom I had led into danger, lest he should be crushed to death. I writhed and struggled in desperation beneath the suffocating pressure. I got out, and comprehended, in a glance, the whole extent of the danger, and my utter inability to release him, ere it would be too late to save him; and I saw, too, that now I was out, the whole weight would settle on him, and crush him. I burst out at the door, mounted the fence, and cried out,

"Miles is under the cart! Miles is under the cart!" The agony of my cry instantly brought my mother and the girl running from the house, and my brother from the field. My mother reached the barn and saw the danger, and went to throwing off the sheaves of wheat; but it would have been too late to save him, but for the assistance of a stranger, who was, at the moment of my cry, passing along the road. He knew that something was the matter, from the agony of my tone; he leaped from his horse, and ran, and reached the barn soon after my step-mother. He saw the danger, and instantly sprang up to the end of the cart pole, and pulled down with might and main, while my mother, the girl, and I, lifted up behind. The cart rose from my brother's chest; my mother snatched him out, and laid him on her lap at the door. He did not breathe; the blood had settled about his eyes and under his nails. His eyes were closed. He was warm, but lay as one dead. By this time, my brothers had come up. We rubbed him, rolled him over, and threw water into his face. After a few moments he breathed, opened his eyes, began to moan, and finally to cry out. My brother was saved alive. The joy of my heart was indescribable. I could not shed a tear while he lay under the cart, nor when I saw him lying in my mother's arms as dead; but when I saw him open his eyes, and that he was actually to live, my heart was too full; I cried for joy, for I felt that the weight of his death was taken off from me. I never led him into danger after this. This is the only instance of danger happening to the life or limb of any child committed to my care.

An instance of generous, sisterly affection often occurred in the school which I attended during the summer of my ninth year, which I used greatly to admire, and which has been most beneficial in its influence. A girl about my own age, named Nancy, came to the same school. Two sisters and a brother younger than herself, came with her. Over all these, she watched with affectionate solicitude, ever following them and watching over them to guard them from all harm. No matter from what source or what cause suffering to them approached, Nancy was sure to stand between them and it; and as she was kindly and good to all the children, and a general favorite, all, by mutual consent, abstained from annoying her little sisters and brother. The brother, whose name was James, who was younger than she, and a lively, careless, restless little fellow, and always running up accounts to be settled by the teacher, was saved from many a punishment by the intervention of his sister. He was just one of those good-natured, forgetful, pliable, restless children, who are most difficult of all to bring into the traces of propriety, and to be kept there; and who are ever going astray and always sorry for it. He was just the amiable child whom every body loved, having no fixedness of will or character, and yielding to whatever influence happened to bear upon him at the moment; one of those children who are most difficult to manage, and for whom parents have most cause to be anxious.

This said boy was always violating the rules of the school, and whenever the teacher spoke to him about it, he at once would acknowledge the fault, appear sincerely penitent, and promise never to do so again. It was counted a great disgrace in that school to be reproved or "spoken to," as we termed it—this disgrace was often visited upon restless, kind-hearted James. At such times, Nancy would suffer far more than he did, and often put in some excuse for him, and the teacher often spared her rebukes for her sake. But little James was often called out before the school to stand beside the teacher, and there receive a long homily on good behavior. At such times, Nancy always stood by his side, holding his hand or putting her arm around him to comfort him by her sympathy, and to excuse his conduct; and if the teacher decided that he must stand in one corner, or in the middle of the floor; or on the table, or be shut up in a dark closet, or sit on the floor under the table, or on a stool at her feet, with the fool's cap on his head—or if she decided to inflict the severer punishment of the ferule or the whip, his generous sister entreated that the punishment, whatever it was to be, might be inflicted on her. Many times have I witnessed the sobbings and tears of anguish in that loving, noble little girl, pleading that the blows might fall on her, and not on her brother. James was ever truthful, and would never seek to escape by denying a fault, nor would his sister thus seek to screen him; but she would grant that he had done wrong, and that he deserved to be punished, and then plead that she might be punished in his stead. Often did the whole school from mere sympathy with the self-forgetting spirit of that sister, join in her entreaties that James might be spared, and we often succeeded in getting him clear.

But Nancy's self-forgetfulness was not confined to her brother. There was scarce a child in that school who did not feel it more or less, and for whom she did not offer herself as a substitute, when punishment was impending. She seemed to consider herself as specially called upon to receive the stripes due to the whole school. It seemed to be her privilege and prerogative, in her own estimation, to suffer for all the rest of us. Of course, the teacher was too truly just and kind ever to inflict upon the generous girl punishment due to others, but many a delinquent was spared for her sake. I have known that girl to stand before the teacher with her arm lovingly thrown around some playmate, and with tears pleading with her to spare the delinquent, or to inflict on herself the penalty. Her loving spirit powerfully affected that whole school; and I believe every child in it was more guarded, and careful not to offend against the rules, for fear of bringing sorrow to her heart. Hers was a martyr spirit. She was loved and honored by all; and to cause sorrow to her heart, or bring tears into her eyes, was counted no trifling offence in the estimation of the children. . . .

Far different from the influence of that girl was the influence of two boys who were, for several years, my schoolfellows. They were about my own age. I never had much contention with either of these boys myself; but scarce a day passed at school, in which they did not fight with each other, and being about equally matched in strength, sometimes one triumphed, and sometimes the other. Their conflicts were cruel, and often bloody; and he who could give the other the most numerous and the blackest bruises was considered the honorable and triumphant champion. They were seldom without bruises. Neither ever complained of the other, to get him punished at school or at home; yet they were often punished by teachers and parents for quarrelling. It was of no use; the next time they met, the very fact that they had been whipped for fighting, by their parents or teachers, would be the occasion of a renewed combat. It was with them a regular beating and battering of eyes and noses, pulling ears, biting, scratching and kicking; and in every way, without using stones or clubs, bruising and wounding each other's flesh. A word or a look was often the cause of a battle between them; and they displayed the same spirit of deadly animosity in their contests, which two nations show when they go to war, and spend millions of money, and destroy thousands of lives, for no better cause. . . .

I cannot forget how I felt when I first saw those two boys fighting and beating each other with their fists. My feelings were greatly shocked; I interfered to part them, at which they were both offended, and which caused them both to turn upon me and strike me. One of them struck me with a club on the forehead, but I did not strike him back with my fist. Having no idea at that time of returning good for evil, or kindness for cruelty, I boxed his ears with my open hand till he cried out. But ever after, I let them fight their battles without an attempt to separate them. It was long, however, before I could see them fight without a feeling of shuddering lest they should put out each other's eyes or kill each other. I could never, as other children did, both boys and girls, urge them on to fight, and shout to one or the other, as the fancy took, to "pitch into" his opponent; but I came to look on their battles with indifference, if not with approbation. Even an elder sister of one of those boys used to put him up to fight the other, to urge him to persevere in the conflict, and to exult with him when he came off victorious. . . .

One of my teachers in childhood was a man of whom my recollections as a teacher are most disagreeable; and whose influence was most pernicious. From some cause, I know not what, he seemed to have a spite towards me, and to exercise many petty cruelties upon me. He pinched and pulled my ears, snapped and thumped my head, and knocked it against the side of the room; he pulled my hair, boxed my ears, slapped my hands with a heavy ferule, and almost daily exercised some petty, spiteful violence upon my person; and often without pretending to name any cause for so doing. I entered no complaints to my father, or to any one; yet I cherished a deep sense of his injustice in my heart, and vowed to myself, if ever I was strong enough, I would beat and bruise him to my heart's content. I did grow strong enough to do it, and met him in his own house, and made known to him my vow of childhood many years after it was made; and asked him if he was ready to be operated upon by the spirit which his conduct towards me in the school had excited in me. He laugh-

ingly pleaded that he had rather be excused; but acknowl-
edged that his treatment of me was just fitted to foster the
spirit of revenge and violence in my heart. . . .

When it was established as a law in the family, or in the
school, that I was to be whipped if I did certain acts or
said certain words, so far from being restrained by a law
sanctioned by such a penalty, it only excited me to do or
say what was forbidden.

For instance: it was a rule in my father's discipline,
that, if his children pushed one another into the snow in
winter in going to or returning from school, he would
whip us. I threw one of my brothers into the snow one
evening, in returning from school, and filled his neck and
bosom full of it. When I had done it, I began to think of
the consequences. My brother, as I let him up, would not
allow me to brush the snow from his clothes, but ran
home and told my father what I had done; and though he
knew, and my father knew, it was done in fun and frolic,
without a thought or feeling of unkindness, in the evening
I had my whipping. What good did it do? The very next
evening, I did the same again; and after this fashion.

There was a deep snow drift a short distance from the
house. As we were coming from school, and passing the
drift, I suddenly tripped my brother, and tumbled him
head foremost into the snow. I then fell upon him, rubbed
the snow into his face, his hair, stuffed it into his neck and
bosom, and filled his pockets and his hat full of snow. I
then let him up, and again he ran home and told my
father. I walked resolutely and deliberately home, my
mind being fully made up and prepared for another whipping. My father met me, and spoke to me kindly, but in a
manner so cool, deliberate and measured, that I saw that I
had no hope of escape. Though not one word was said to
me about the matter; though my father seemed very particularly kind to me, and my brother and I were on as

good and loving terms as ever, yet I seemed to see the whip in my father's eye, and to hear it in his cool, low, determined voice, and to feel it in his heart. But not one word was said about it that night. There was an influence that drew me irresistibly towards him that evening, and led me to be officious in my offers of assistance, as he was packing up and getting ready for a distant journey. All my offers he kindly received, but still in a cool, collected, and ominous way. I went to bed without the whipping; but not to sleep, for I was thinking, thinking about it. The next morning I was up early to see my father off. He had his breakfast, read his chapter, and said his prayers in his family. The horses were harnessed and at the door, and my father was putting on his overcoat, and not one word had he yet said to me about the whipping. I wondered, but was not allowed for a moment to suppose that he had forgotten it, for I saw too plainly the whip in his calm, determined face, and in his decided, though kind voice, whenever he looked at me or spoke to me. He put on his hat and mittens, and took his whip and went to the door, and I followed, keeping close to him. He took the reins, and as he was stepping into his sleigh, he turned and whispered to me, in a distinct, calm, and determined tone, "Henry, I'll settle with you when I come back." He drove off, and my heart died within me. He was gone two weeks, during which time I was in torment; restless, sleepless, and without relish for food. A thousand actual whippings would have been as nothing compared to what I experienced in the certain prospect of one. At length, the earnestly longed-for day of his return came round. I watched with feverish excitement his coming. He came in sight, drove up to the house, and stopped, and the first words I spoke to him were to entreat him to whip me. Soon as convenient he did so; not sparing one jot or tittle of the sum total, out of regard to what I had already suffered.

Those were the last blows my father ever struck me, though he lived many years, to see me come to man's estate. But it was not the violence that did me good; it was the mental anguish and the mastery acquired over my own spirit by those two weeks' suspense and expectation.

The contrast to that cruel, provoking teacher was a female teacher. She never laid the hand of violence upon me during the five months I was under her care and seldom did she strike one of her scholars. She had a far more efficient way of keeping order in her school. She was calm, collected, affectionate, but firm and undeviating in her manner; spoke to us in a low, distinct, decided, but sweet and kindly tone of voice; never threatened, and altogether treated the children in a way to win their affection and confidence. We all loved that teacher, for we felt that she loved us, and that she sought and acted for our good in all she did. That summer's school was one of the brightest spots of childhood, for there all that was gentle, loving and happy in my nature was brought into exercise; and many times, since I came to understand the power of love and kindness over hatred and cruelty, have I turned to that teacher and her school, as an illustration of the truth that Love Begets Love, gentleness, gentleness; while I have turned to other teachers, as illustrations of the equally known and established truth, that Violence Begets Violence.

There was one kind of punishment which one of my teachers used to inflict on boys, which has often seemed to me of more than questionable utility. I am certain in some cases it was very hurtful. When any little boy was restive and untractable, she would seat him between two girls as a punishment. It was called "sitting between the girls" by the teacher and the scholars; and this came to be a most hateful and dreaded penalty in that school, for it invariably made the delinquent the butt of ridicule to all the scholars, both girls and boys. And by way of enhancing the shame and the disgrace to any guilty of very gross misconduct, each of the two girls was to put an arm around his neck or body. This punishment seldom failed to humble any obstinate boy, and to lead him to mend his manners; for it was so managed, in the administration of it, that it never failed to excite the ridicule and reproach of the whole school against the delinquent, and that without one particle of sympathy in his favor; for no one felt that there could be any great danger of physical suffering to be made to sit between two girls, with their arms around him; yet every one felt it would be a grievous shame and penalty to be obliged to sit there, and a thing of which he would not soon hear the end. Whatever effect this might have had to keep order in the school, it certainly led to a most unhappy state of feeling in the boys toward the girls. The boys felt that the supposed superior dignity of their sex was compromised and insulted by it; and though they joined with the girls in reproaching the victim, yet, on the whole, it had a decided tendency to make the boys unkind and ungentle towards the girls. It made them ashamed to be seen in company with the girls; ashamed to be seen playing with them, or rendering them any act of brotherly regard and assistance. I believe it had the effect to confirm the boys in the belief that, by the virtue of their being boys, they were superior to the girls; and that there was more dignity and more glory in being a boy than in being a girl. It was often sad to see little brothers running away from their younger sisters; leaving them in tears, to wander home alone, because they were ashamed to be seen walking with them, leading them by the hand, helping them along, and encouraging them to encounter any supposed dangers of the woods. Not unfrequently were brothers punished by their parents, and by the teacher, for thus deserting their young sisters; but generally to little effect. The foolish and wicked taunts of their school-fellows had more weight with them in this matter, than the authority of parents or teacher. The taunt of being a "girl-boy," as he was jeeringly called who had to sit between the girls, or who was seen to lead a little sister by the hand, and to be affectionately kind to her, was all-potent with most of the boys, to make them uncourteous and unkind to the girls. It is a mean and wicked feeling, and when any little boy is superior in strength of body to his little sisters, he will not, if he is truly noble and generous, seek to make them feel their inferiority by being ashamed to walk with them, and to be kind to them; he will not run away from them, and leave them to their sorrows and helplessness, but will stand by them, to comfort and sustain them by his energy and hardihood, and to make their way in life easy and happy.

My little, restless, fidgety, kind-hearted brother used often to get between the girls; and their arms in great glee twined around him. Unfortunate boy! He used to roar lustily, as the laughing girls would hold him between them, and the whole school would be tittering over him. He would struggle and roar, but to no purpose; there he was held down. I used to feel for the sufferings of that little fellow, while undergoing torments; but I could not help him, except by shielding him from the taunts of the boys afterwards; which I often did effectually, by turning the feelings of the boys against the girls. But no monarch's heart ever swelled with indignation at an insult to his dignity, as did that little brother's with a sense of the indignity and dishonor put upon him, as a boy, by the treatment of the girls. The two girls between whom the culprit was to sit were always named by the teacher; and this punishment had well-nigh set my brother against the whole sex. One thing I could not account for; that teacher never punished a delinquent girl by seating her between two boys. I know not why.

I had not naturally a cruel disposition, for I never could endure to see even animals in pain, much less my fellow creatures; and when theology teaches (Christianity never taught it) that human nature is more prone to cruelty than to kindness, I know it is not true in reference to myself; nor do I believe it is true of men generally. No possible amount of evidence could make me believe a theological dogma which is opposed to this innate conviction of my heart, and to the experience of my whole life.

Yet I have been cruel to animals and to human beings. I was trained to the feeling and practice of violence towards animals, as the only mode of subjecting them to my will. I now see that gentleness has a more subduing and beneficial effect than harshness, not only upon beasts, but on human beings.

My father made his own pork, as well as his beef, on his own farm—a universal practice in that region. I was sent one day to feed the pigs. There was one, the largest and finest looking in the drove, which was determined to have all to himself, and which showed a savage temper towards his fellow pigs. I was aroused by the selfishness of the brute, and its cruelty to the smaller and weaker ones. I caught up a stone and hurled it at him. It was aimed with fatal precision for the comfort of the poor beast. It hit him in the face. The poor creature sent up a cry of agony and ran. It soon stopped, lay down, rolled about in its agony, and then started off again. Thus it continued to manifest its distress for half an hour. It finally came back to the rest, lay down, and moaned piteously. It was then I saw what I had done. I had knocked out his eye, and the blood was pouring from the empty socket, and the eye was hanging two or three inches below it by a cord. I felt grieved by the pain I had inflicted upon the poor beast, and resolved to throw no more stones at the pigs.

On one occasion, I found a sparrow's nest on my way to school, near the road-side, but well sheltered. There were several eggs in it. I visited that nest twice a day, and often left crumbs of bread by it for the bird to eat. The sparrow became familiar with me, and would seldom fly away at my approach. The process of hatching was accomplished, and four tender young ones appeared. I paid my daily visits, and left some food. The young birds grew apace. They were nearly fledged. One evening, returning from school, I took one of the young ones in my hand. It screamed for fright. The mother-bird flew at me in great excitement. I caught up a stone and hurled it at her, and killed her. My first thought, on picking up that dead mother-bird in one hand, while I held one of the bereaved and now doomed young ones in the other, was "Not a sparrow falls to the ground without His notice." Then it rushed upon my mind, "What will He think of this wanton cruelty?" This was the first feeling of deep remorse I remember to have experienced. I put the helpless young bird into the nest; it nestled down with the other little ones. I sat down by them, looked at them and their dead mother, and I wept over what I had done. I finally comforted myself with the hope that the cock sparrow would feed and cherish them. I went home; and that was a sad night. My heart ached for the young birds, lest they should be exposed to the night air and die. As I passed to school next morning, I visited the nest. My worst fears were realized. The tender birds lay huddled together, *dead*. They had no mother-bird to protect them from the night air, and they were chilled to death. I sat down by those birds and wept, for my heart was full. I buried them, and long after did I remember that spot.

This little incident has held back my hand from many strong temptations to throw stones at birds. This, and the incident of the pig, gave a powerful check to my habit of cruelty to animals and birds; and sure I am, my reflections on them have greatly tended to foster in me a spirit of gentleness toward human beings.

II

Of my father's twelve children that lived to grow up, all but one could sing, and most of them could play on instruments of various kinds. I have no recollection of the time when I could not sing. The first tunes and hymns I remember to have learned, were some Baptist and Methodist hymns set to music. I had a clear alto voice, and can remember, as among my earliest impressions, singing these hymns to my oldest brother, and hearing him praise my singing. Early in life, I began to play on musical instruments; especially upon the fife and the flute. I had four brothers who could play on various instruments. We could play the fife, the flute, the hautboy [oboe], the clarionet [*sic*], the bassoon, the kettle drum, and the bass drum. My father was a good bass singer. Often were we all at home at a family concert, and often have I accompanied my older brothers, and played with them on parade days. When quite young, I have played on the fife for military companies on review days, and received two dollars per day and my keeping. But my greatest delight in music was when singing or playing by myself, or with my brothers. In my childhood and youth, and to the present day, there is no instrumental music so sweet and elevating to my mind as that produced by the bugle, when it is skilfully played. Its tones cast a spell over my feelings, which I never could express.

As a child I attended a singing school, and sang the alto, or counter; and I learned to read music, and to sing tunes and words which I never before saw or heard, with much facility. My taste for music was not cultivated to any great extent. It may not have been very nice and discriminating; but such as it was, it was innate, and not the work of human teachings. My love for playing on instruments, and for humming over tunes in solitude, with only my own thoughts and feelings to keep me company, has exercised a powerful control over my heart and life, and has kept me away from many social temptations.

I never could discern the difference commonly made between sacred and profane music. It was a mystery to me, when a child, why "Yankee Doodle" should be called profane, and "Old Hundred" sacred. I might take Watt's *Psalms and Hymns*, and sing any thing in that book, to a proper tune on Sunday; but to sing "Bonny Doon," or "Mary in Heaven," would have been counted wrong. I had many speculations about this distinction. . . .

My father taught his children to regard the first day of the week as the Lord's day. Of course, the impression was deep and abiding on my mind, that other days were not the Lord's days, and that it was not so easy to desecrate the other days as it was the first. It never entered my mind that any other day than that could be desecrated. Do what I would on other days; jump, wrestle, play ball, climb trees, laugh, shout, or wander about the meadows, pastures, or woods, picking berries, looking at the birds and squirrels—no wrong was done to the day. I never could feel that doing these things desecrated my body or soul on any day; but I was taught to believe that, while my heavenly Father was pleased to see me do these things on other days, He was displeased to see me do them on

Sunday. Often have I been rebuked for laughing and merriment on Sunday, and for looking out of the window. But I could not understand how an act that did not injure me, nor my fellow men, could insult or injure the Deity on that day. No one ever explained this to me, when I was a child; nor has any one explained it to me since.

I had a sabbatarian feeling—a first day religion; and I often used to condemn myself when I found my thoughts wandering, on the Sabbath, to the green fields and woods of summer, or to a slide down hill in winter; but I could not help it. I used to try very hard to be good, and to keep my restless, merry thoughts from wandering on Sunday; but it was of no use; they would rove about the pastures and meadows, and in the woods; and I never thought of condemning myself for it; but I thought I must feel, and did often feel, very unhappy, because I could not stop feeling and thinking. I never could see how it was a greater wrong to lie, to steal, get drunk, or do any wicked thing on the Sabbath, than on any other day; yet I was told it was. The only reason given why I must not look out of the window, or go about the meadows and woods on the first day of the week, was, "it is Sunday, the Lord's holy day"; and how Sunday could make wrong what Monday made right, I could not tell; yet, on the authority of others, I thought it must be so.

My father kept his Sabbath from sundown to sundown. As soon as the sun was set Saturday night, all work and play were suspended; and a new aspect came upon the family. This Sabbath-day look, tone and manner were kept up till the sun set on Sunday evening; and then the family assumed its laughing, talking, busy appearance. I was allowed to sing and play, and run about as I pleased. Many times have I watched the hands of the clock, or the setting sun, with longing eyes, to catch the first moment when it would be right to do these things. My brothers and sisters would then go off to their amusements; and the restraints were taken away the moment the hands of the clock pointed to a particular hour and minute on the dial. I could not see into it, and no one could enlighten me upon it then; no one ever has. . . .

Going to meeting on Sunday was as much a part of my father's life as his daily bread. It was in his view a duty from which none were absolved. The meeting to which he belonged [Hartwick Congregational Church which he joined in 1800] was four miles from his house; and, rain or shine, summer or winter, hot or cold, he usually went to meeting, and took some of his family with him. The great wagon, or sleigh, was taken out; the horses were harnessed to it, and brought round to the door, and there my father and mother, and as many children as could pack in, were loaded into the wagon, and driven to meeting. Even the horses and the dog seemed to know when the family were going to meeting. Those who could not get into the wagon walked. The road to meeting ran up a valley, beside the Otsego creek; a delightful ride. The meeting-house was small and dingy; large enough, however, for all who came. It was usually called "the house of God." I never could tell why it should be called "God's house," while others were not. I used to ask myself if God did not dwell in my father's house as well as in the meeting-house. My father owned a pew in front of the high pulpit, in which he and the older children used to sit; and the younger ones were sent up into the gallery, to sit where and how they pleased; my father not thinking that, if any of his children needed his care, the younger ones did. But we were taught the mysteries of sitting still in the meeting-house, as well as in the school-house. There we sat, and heard the singing, the praying, the preaching and the benediction, as silently, worshipfully and wakefully as we could; though many a sound nap did the parents and children take in that old meeting-house in hot weather; and many a time did they shiver and shake, and look blue, in winter, for there was no stove nor fire, and the thermometer was sometimes down to zero; and the people must have extraordinary zeal to keep comfortable, sitting still in meeting in such an atmosphere. Soon as the minister had said his last "Amen," the children in the gallery rushed for the door, glad to be relieved from the confinement. We entered the wagon, drove home, put up the horses, and then sat still in the house till sundown.

There were two whiskey shops in that village [Hartwick], near the meeting-house; both kept by persons who were members of the church to which my father belonged. The men used to gather into these whiskey shops between divine service, smoke cigars and pipes, and drink whiskey, and discuss over the affairs of their farms; nor could I see any more harm in these things, than in singing, praying and preaching. They would then go to the meeting-house again at the appointed time. They went from the performance of religious service, in the meeting-house, to the secular service of drinking whiskey, and smoking tobacco, in the whiskey shops; and then back again to the meeting-house to their divine performances. These gatherings in the whiskey shops, at noon, to drink whiskey, smoke tobacco, and talk over the price of pigs, &c., were as intimately associated with going to meeting, as part and parcel of Sunday's service, as were the performances in the meeting-house.

Rove, a great black dog of my father's, used to perform his part of the Sunday service on this wise: In going to meeting, he went before, and cleared the road of hens, geese, pigs and cattle. While the family were at their worship in the meeting-house, he would lie in the carriage to watch it; broiling under the summer's sun, or shivering beneath the cold blasts of winter. Then, as we started for home, he would usually leap into somebody's wood-yard and seize a stick of wood, or a stake or rail from some fence, and march before the horses—carrying his burden in his mouth till he reached home. Rove was a wayward, reckless dog; and many a dog, goose, pig, cow and wood-pile had cause to remember him. But he regularly went to meeting.

Such are my childhood's recollections of going to meeting. I certainly regarded it, at that time, as a religious act in itself, pleasing to God. Going to meeting was something that must be done, and all my recollections of it are connected with it as an observance. I am certain I had little or no idea of going to meeting to learn how to treat my parents, brothers and sisters and playmates more kindly. I certainly had no thought that it had any connection with my life at home, in the school or on the play-ground; and as a general thing, I do not believe that it had any redeeming influence on my feelings or my conduct, during the week. The observance, in my mind, was wholly confined to the Sabbath.

The only thing required to be remembered was the text; and it was the custom of my father to require his children to find the text, after we reached home, and learn to repeat it to him. This remembering the text, and the chapter and verse of it, was intimately associated in my mind with meeting-going; the only thing I thought of bringing away from the meeting was the text. Seldom did any one attempt to call to my mind, during the week, what the minister said on the Sabbath; nor was I shown to apply the instructions given from the pulpit to the regulation of my heart and conduct in the plays and labors of the week. . . .

I was regularly taught the Westminster Catechism once a week. It was called—"saying the Catechism." It was done after this fashion: Soon as we came from meeting,

Sunday afternoon, and the horses were unharnessed and put to stable or pasture, and the Sunday clothes taken off, folded and laid aside, and our ordinary clothes put on, and the whole process of meeting-going finished, my father seated us around the room. Then he, being seated where he could have an eye upon us all, took the Catechism and began to put the questions, beginning with— "What is the chief end of man?"—then going on with the questions to the end. Each answered a question; or, if he could not do it correctly, it was put to the next. We all had to sit still, while "saying the Catechism." Not a whisper, nor a movement, passed unrebuked. It was a serious and solemn performance, and every feeling and look must be regulated accordingly. But I said the Catechism as a parrot repeats words. I do not recollect that any explanations, or practical applications, were made of a single question or answer. I used to wonder what was meant by "Effectual Calling," "Original Sin," "Under Grace," and many other phrases in that Catechism; but no one told me; and I do not believe that any other faculty was ever called into activity, while saying it, but my memory. My heart, my affections, were untouched by the process. My conscience was unenlightened; my reasoning powers lay dormant, except it were to doubt; and my imagination not aroused, except to wonder what this or that meant; but there I sat, in stolid, silent, and often miserable solemnness, repeating words with which I associated nothing but weary emptiness. . . .

I was taught to reverence every chapter and verse in the Bible as the Word of God, and to believe that when I was reading any part of it, I was conversing with the Deity. The Bible had to be read on Sunday. Each child that could read, must read his chapter during the day. This Sunday-reading of a chapter was a duty which was not to be omitted. The children were to take the Bible, and read to themselves or aloud, more reverently than other books were read. Reading the chapter was the task to be performed; and little concern was manifested as to what impressions were made, what feelings engendered, or what thoughts awakened.

These Sunday Bible-readings powerfully affected my mind, and I imbibed a profound veneration for the book; not for the sentiments it contained. These, I know, were not the source of my sacred regard for it; but I thought the book was a holy book, as I thought the Sabbath was a holy day, and the meeting-house a holy house, and therefore I reverenced it. I regarded it as God's book, as I did the Sabbath and meeting-house, God's day and house; and when I took it into my hand, I felt more awe-stricken than when I handled any other book; and I opened and read it with a feeling that there was more virtue, in opening and reading it, than any other. . . .

Praying in the family, which my father called "doing duty," was done in this manner. The children were called in, before breakfast, wherever they were, if within hailing distance. The gathering call was, "Come to duty," or, "Come to prayers." All came into the room, and were seated in silence. A mysterious dread was often on my mind on such occasions; and to this day, that call, "Come to duty," has an undefinable solemnity connected with it. After we were all seated, and my father had taken down and opened the great family Bible, and adjusted his spectacles, he began to read from the sermon on the mount; or about the killing of Achan and his little children, or the men, women, and infants of Jericho; or Samuel hewing Agag to pieces before the Lord; or Samson killing the Philistines; for he read chapter after chapter, verse after verse, in course; believing every verse and chapter to be the word of God, and given for instruction and edification. After reading the chapter, he stood up, and we all arose, each in his place; and he, generally standing in the same spot, began to pray. His prayer was the same, morning and evening, with slight alterations, and uttered in a deliberate and solemn tone and manner. He ended, and we at once became as usual. We began to talk and busy ourselves about ordinary avocations, as though no extraordinary thing had been transpiring before us.

Yet, my father and his family regarded "tending duty" as an affair of importance and solemnity. There was more solemn preparation for this than for any other business done in the family; why, I could not tell then, nor can I now. There was to be no looking out of the window upon the bright, sunny morn, or the earth sparkling with dew; no winks, looks or nods between the children, no smiles, nor suppressed whisperings; but a dead silence and a chilling solemnity were to be put on for that occasion. Had these family scenes been associated with more cheerfulness and loving familiarity, very different had been their influence on me.

The impression made on my mind by these stated family exercises in praying was deep and abiding. When my thoughts were not preoccupied by some scheme of amusement or labor, and I could give them, as I sometimes did, to what was passing before me, I regarded my father with a feeling of awe. Often have I looked at him with astonishment. There he stood, his back towards us, his face to the wall, leaving his hands on the top of a chair, talking in a solemn, deliberate and earnest tone of voice to a "Being" whom I could not see. . . .

I used sometimes to hear a neighbor praying in the woods, in a very loud voice. He would always do this on his knees under some tree, and I have crept softly near enough to him, and gazed at him with amazement from behind a tree. It used to perplex me greatly, whether he saw any thing in the top of the tree, for his face would be turned up. There was a Methodist Elder in the same town. He was a very zealous preacher, of an ardent, enthusiastic temperament, and often passed our house to go to his preaching on the mountain east of us. When, in ascending the hill through the woods, he reached a certain spot, he usually alighted from his horse, and knelt down beside the road and prayed; and in a voice so loud that we could often hear him half a mile distant in the valley below. That man's voice used to echo around the deep forest like a trumpet. I used to be amazed at this, and wonder if prayer, when said in the woods, and in such a loud voice, was more likely to be heard and accepted by God, and more profitable to those who said it.

This Elder was an object of sacred dread to me, and the following incident greatly increased this feeling towards him. He was sick of fever. One Sunday morning, when the fever was near a crisis, he insisted that his family should leave him alone, and go to meeting. He was so earnest and restless about it, that they complied. When they had departed, he arose, went down to a spring of icy coldness, near the house, and there plunged into it. He bathed to his heart's content; then came back to his room, dressed, and sat down by a fire, and was found sitting there, his fever gone, and all danger passed. He sent word all over the region that he would hold a meeting in the schoolhouse near by, on a certain evening, and there tell what a miracle had been wrought on him. The night and the meeting came. I was there, with other members of the family. The Elder appeared, looking thin and pale; but he was well. He arose in the midst, and told the whole process; how it was revealed to him to go to the spring and bathe; how he was strengthened to walk down to it; the sudden effect of the cold water; the disappearance of the fever, and the sudden increase of strength. He really believed that he had been an object of Heaven's special visitation, and he became more earnest and loud in his prayers as he ascended that hill in the woods, than ever, and he became an object of an increased dread to me. . . .

I was taught two prayers, when very young, by my father—the Lord's prayer, and the following:—

> "Now I lay me down to sleep,
> I pray the Lord my soul to keep;
> If I should die before I wake,
> I pray the Lord my soul to take."

But I never was made to go by myself to say these prayers morning and evening; nor was I made to kneel by my father, and say them to him. . . .

I look back with a feeling of deep and affectionate interest upon those Sabbath observances, meeting-goings, catechisings, Bible-readings and prayers of my father. They serve to endear his memory to my heart; for, though I believe he was mistaken in the views which he took of these things, and the manner of his doing them, yet, I felt then, and do still feel assured, that he had the best interests of his children at heart, and only wished to influence them to love their God and to keep His Commandments.

There was a kind of sacred feeling associated in my mind with the word "Church,"—and with the phrase—"Joining a Church,"—and I supposed that people who joined a church were, by some mysterious influence, taken from the company of the evil, and put into the company of the good, and that they had a prescriptive right to heaven. I never thought it was necessary for myself or any one, to refrain from fretting, scolding, and fighting; or that we must be just, honest, kind and loving, in order to join a church; but, I did have an idea that I must not go to parties nor dance, nor laugh, run, shout and play, if I joined a church. This act, I thought, would put an end to all that constituted life to me. Yet, I meant to join a church at some future time, in order to make sure of heaven. Though I was convinced that I must join a church, or never have heaven, yet I determined to put it off as long as I could. I felt by turns a spirit of joyous activity on the play-ground, and a sweet, tranquil, delightful feeling in the company of my little sisters, or in my wanderings in the woods, which seemed to me perfectly innocent and delightful, but which I supposed I must put away, if I joined a church.

Often, when I have seen infants brought up to be baptized, have I wondered what good it could do them; and, when the minister sprinkled water in their faces, and said over them the accustomed formula, I have looked on with a kind of stupid wonder, how that could benefit the child, or make it acceptable to God; and the mystery has never been solved. When I have seen men and women led down into the river, and plunged under the water and seen them rise up gasping and strangling for breath, as I often did, and was told God was pleased with this, and that it was confessing Christ before men, I used to get bewildered; for I could not see how it could be any more pleasing to God, or profitable to themselves, to have a minister plunge them under the water, than to plunge themselves under as they did in swimming, or to be plunged in by any body that was not a minister.

Often have I sat and seen my father and others celebrate the sacrament or supper, with an indefinable feeling of awe. It was said, that they were eating the body and drinking the blood of Christ, as they took bits of bread and ate them, and the cup and drank wine; and I have felt the sense of fear come over me as I have seen them do these things. I used to marvel how eating that bit of bread, and tasting that drop of wine, when they were neither hungry nor thirsty, could please God. I never supposed that it could be of any use to them, by sustaining their bodies, or by purifying their souls, or my making them live more just and honest lives. Yet I thought that these observances were a necessary part of religion.

My childhood's impressions about *conversion* were that it was some mysterious operation performed upon the soul by an unseen agent. I supposed that it was to be done suddenly; and to be begun and ended in one and the same moment. I thought that it must be preceded by a great deal of anguish of mind; by many sighs and groans; and by visits from the minister and church-members, to talk with me about my soul. This antecedent process was called, "conviction, or distress of mind." Many times in the family, on the play-ground, in the school and in the church, when I felt serious, have I put on a careless, cheerful air and manner, lest I should be thought to be "under distress of mind." I greatly dreaded being thought to be passing through this initiatory step to conversion. I had no doubt that I must one day go through it, but I wanted to put it off as long as I could.

After being under distress of mind, for a time, then, all at once, came the conversion. This operation consisted in a sudden change from distress to joy; and this was all I supposed to be meant by "old things passing away; and all things becoming new," and by "putting off the old man, and putting on the new."

Before people joined the church, it was customary to have them come out before the congregation in the meeting-house, and tell their experience. This consisted almost universally in telling how they had been "under distress of mind"; how deeply and how long they suffered before conversion came; what first threw them into this distress, which was often some dream, or vision, or death, or sermon, or prayer, or remark, or text, flashing suddenly upon them. Then came a sudden rebound of the spirit, the shoutings and hallelujahs. I have heard many of these new converts relate their experience in my childhood, and it usually consisted in passing through the above process.

The Methodists held a camp-meeting in some woods near my father's. The camp was formed in a beautiful spot—in a forest of tall trees, and at the foot of a high hill. The underbrush and bushes were cleared away from about an acre—the trees were left standing. The old logs and brushwood were taken away; and the cleared spot was enclosed by a brush fence, not easily penetrated by man or beast. There were two gates, one for the public to enter,—and the other for private entrance, and retirement of the preachers. A high scaffolding was erected near the entrance gate, for the preachers' stand. In front of it was a platform; before the platform was a little pen or fold, into which the anxious inquirers were put.

To this meeting came the Methodists from thirty or forty miles around; bringing their tents, beds and provisions with them. The tents were put up around inside the enclosure; and sometimes several families were in a tent. Here they remained in the camp, men, women and children—singing, praying, preaching, shouting, exhorting, day and night, for a week; having several sermons every day and every night.

I was there two days and one night; spending the night in the tent of some friends. It was the first I ever attended. What I there saw and heard deeply affected my spirit. Within the camp, convictions and conversions were going on night and day. The singing, by night, was most impressive, as it rose and died away in those dark woods; but all around the camp, outside of the enclosure, was carried on every species of wickedness. Gingerbread and whiskey carts, and shows of various kinds, were there, and the noise of revelry, drunkenness and blasphemy mingled with the singing, praying, and preaching. That was a fearful night to me, as I wandered about in that camp—the bright watch-fires and candles making the darkness and gloom of the forest more dark and gloomy.

But I was most affected by what took place to one of my play-fellows. It was about midnight. Here and there all about the camp, groups or classes were formed to pray and sing. I had been standing near one, leaning against a tree, and looking upon about fifty men and women—many of whom I knew—as they knelt together praying; many of them at the same time shouting, "Amen," "Glory," Alleluia," and striking their hands together. These people I really supposed were worshipping God, and doing Him acceptable service. My attention was called to the minister's place of operation by unusual shouting and earnest praying. I went up and looked into the "anxious pen," and there, to my amazement, I saw one of my school-fellows, in the strongest contortions of face and body. Soon I saw him fall flat on the ground, and stretch himself out on his back, looking pale and ghastly; his eyes shut—his hands clenched. There he lay some minutes, as one dead; the preachers all rushing down the steps from the platform, and kneeling around him, shouting, "The great and mighty power of God is on him; pray, brethren, pray for his deliverance." They did pray and shout over him. I was frightened, lest he was dead. He was not a pleasant and happy-tempered boy, and few liked him; but I was afraid the poor fellow was dead, as he lay there, so pale and still, while the ministers were shouting and praying over him. But in the midst of it all, he suddenly sprang to his feet, and began to leap up and down, and clap his hands, and shout out, at the top of his voice, "Glory," "Alleluia," "Praise the Lord," and the like; and the ministers joined in the same shoutings. I was inexpressibly amazed and confounded. What had come over the fellow I could not tell.

They said he had been convicted and converted; but what that meant, I knew not. I crept away into the corner of a tent, and there lay coiled up the rest of the night, thinking of the scene I had witnessed; wondering if I must one day go through such a dreadful operation, in order to be good.

I had no idea conversion meant a practical change from hatred to love, from revenge to forgiveness, from lying to speaking the truth, from cruelty to kindness, from injustice to justice, and from dishonesty to honesty. Nothing that I saw or heard of it gave me any such impression. My sole idea of it was—a sudden mental change, from deep anguish of mind to great happiness.

The minister filled a very large place in my mental vision as a child. But what place did he hold? One of affectionate, confiding regard? No: the minister was the last person on earth in whom, as a child, I could confide, or from whom I felt any tender affection; the last person from whom I could have asked counsel in things pertaining to this world, or to any other. Yet there was no person whom I was taught more to reverence.

I was afraid of them, and I would rather have met a bear, or a wolf, in the woods, alone, than a minister. An indefinable shudder came over me at the thought of meeting one, and of being in his company alone, and of having him speak to me personally.

Nor less did I dread to meet the minister in the family circle. It was the custom for the minister to pay annual or semi-annual visits to the families belonging to his church and congregation, and who contributed to his support. On these occasions, business and all plays were suspended, and the children had to be washed, and dressed in their cleanest and best. It was understood that the minister was coming to have a professional consultation with each member of the family about the health and prospects of his or her soul. This was a thing which I particularly dreaded. At the appointed hour, the family were all seated in readiness for the interview; my father first, then my mother, then the children, from the oldest to the youngest. The minister arrived; came into the room in a solemn manner; sat a moment and looked round, and then asked if all the family were present; and was answered that all were present who were expected to be. He first prayed, and then began to question my father; then my mother; then the oldest child; and so went round the circle, putting questions to each and every one personally. The questions were generally in substance as follows: "What is the state of your soul?" "Is the love of God shed abroad in your heart?" "Have you repented of sin?" "Do you hate sin?" "Do you feel that you are a sinner?" "Do you ever pray?" "Do you try to sanctify the Lord's day, and keep it holy?" As these questions were put, each gave such an answer as was thought appropriate. It was a fiery ordeal, and the sweat has rolled off me as the questioning drew near; and when my turn came, I was so wrought up that I answered at random, yes or no, without knowing or caring whether the answer referred to the question or not. I had a horror of this family visitation and questioning about the state of my soul; yet I regarded it as a thing that must be done.

But I have sometimes ran away from them, and secretly betaken myself to the woods, far out of sight and hearing of the house, and hid in the top of a tree, or in some dark thicket, and there remained for hours, solely to get rid of these consultations about my soul. But I never felt easy when I did so; simply because I supposed this terrible ordeal was something that ought to be and must be passed through, in order to be converted. But it was a heartfelt relief to me when this trial was over for the time being; for I had not a thought that these professional visits had, or were designed to have, the least connection with my feelings and actions in daily life. The consultations related to the concerns of the soul in another state; and these, in my view, had nothing to do with my conduct in this world.

I had not this feeling of horror towards ministers because I supposed they were bad men. On the contrary, I was accustomed to regard them as most devout and holy; and it was precisely because of their supposed piety, that I had such a horror of them; for at that time, piety had no connection with any of those joyous or happy feelings which I experienced in myself. I supposed that if I became pious, all my bright and happy feelings must be put away. . . .

My father always kept whiskey or some kind of spirits in the house; and it was carried into the field and there drank, more or less, in time of haying and harvest. The ploughing, sowing, planting, hoeing, chopping, and other common operations on the farm, were carried on without it, but in haying and harvesting it was always supplied. I never saw my father, or one of my brothers, drunk. They supposed that it was right and necessary to drink, to make them strong, and able to work. Yet I used often to see people drunk, who were hired to help get in our hay and wheat; and it was a marvel to me then, how whiskey, if it made men strong and better able to work, could make them reel and stagger and fall down, and not be able to rise again.

I never liked whiskey, or other intoxicating drinks. I drank it, supposing that I must, because the rest did, but I never liked it. There was a pure brook of delicious water, that ran within a few feet of the door, and a spring of unrivalled clearness, coldness and richness, a few rods further off. These always offered to me a more delicious and tempting beverage. I have often knelt and laid down by that crystal spring, and touched my lips to the water and drank. Often, in the evening, have I gone to it, to get water for the night, and often, during the day, to get it for my brothers at work in the field. That spring is a dear spot in the map of my childhood. Some beech, birch, and pine bushes overhung the dear fountain. No tea, coffee, or chocolate, of which I scarce ever drank, ever tasted so delicious and refreshing as a draught from that spring.

A drunkard was always an object of pity as well as of horror to me. I never could laugh and make merry over his silly, disgusting babblings. I often saw men drunk, for the distilleries were in every neighborhood, and these were the most lucrative markets for the farmer's grain crops, and they took pay partly in whiskey. . . . Tee-totalism was not thought or heard of in the days of my childhood. Whiskey was considered a necessary article of life, and supplied to all families as was bread or meat. It was thought that one could no more be dispensed with than the other.

What were called bees (social gatherings to aid one another) were famous places for manufacturing drunk-ards. It was a new country, *i.e.*, a country covered with native forests. A man bought a tract of this forest land. The first thing to be done was to clear away the trees and open the earth to the sun. These must be cut down with an axe wielded by the hand of man. Often a new settler, wishing to clear a few acres, would invite his neighbors to give him a helping hand to chop down the trees. They would come and give him each a day's work. And such a resounding of the axes as they were struck into the trees; and such a crackling, crashing and roaring as the gigantic sons of the forest made, when they came to the ground! This was a glorious sight to my eyes, and early did I learn to wield the axe and to fell these stately trees. They were felled and cut into pieces, ten or fifteen feet long, the branches also being cut off, and cut into suitable lengths.

This operation, when thus performed gratuitously by the neighbors, was called a chopping bee. The whiskey always circulated freely on these occasions, and limbs were often broken, and sometimes lives destroyed in consequence. Then, after the logs and branches had become dry enough to burn, again were the neighbors invited to come and lend a helping hand; and again they came, with all the horses and oxen that could be mustered. The logs were drawn together and rolled into heaps, and the branches and brush picked up by children and youth, and cast upon the log heaps or into brush heaps. These brush and log heaps, the new settler could burn at his leisure. Thus he could get a piece of ground cleared in a few days, which it would have taken him months to have cleared alone. These gatherings were called logging bees; and these, too, were fruitful occasions of whiskey drinking.

But these chopping and logging bees were occasions of great interest to the young boys all about, and they went with their little axes, and worked manfully at the little trees and bushes, while their fathers and older brothers brought down the tall ones.

Indian corn was extensively grown, and used for bread and puddings, as well as for making whiskey, and for fattening beef and pork. This crop was ready for harvesting in October. If a man had a large crop, and only his own hands to husk it he would cut down the corn with a sickle or scythe, and draw it to some spot, and lay it in heaps— then send round and invite his neighbors, far and near, to come on an appointed evening (for this was usually night work) and help him husk it. The neighbors came, and generally husked till all was done, if it took most of the night. This was all gratuitous. Of course, the whiskey circulated freely; every one helping himself as frequently and as plentifully as he chose. These gatherings were called husking bees, and were frightful sources of drunkenness. Generally, many went away intoxicated.

The houses were built universally of wood at that time, and in that region, and still are to a great extent, throughout America, except in large towns or cities. Carpenters went into the forest, selected trees, felled them, cut them to suitable lengths for the various parts, hewed them, and framed them to fit together. These were all taken to the spot where the building was to stand. Then invitations were sent round to the neighbors to come, on an appointed afternoon, and put up the frame of the building thus made ready. They came, and, under the direction of the master carpenter, put it up, from the foundation to the ridge-pole. This was called a raising bee; and, in these matters, my father and some of my elder brothers had much to do. These raisings were great occasions; and, as the labor was gratuitous, the whiskey went round most freely, and many a serious injury used to be the result. But no matter; the whiskey must go round, or the frame could not go up. These were great sources of drunkenness; for, as at chopping, logging and husking bees, all were expected to drink as often and as plentifully as they pleased.

After the frame was up, the last timber placed, and the last peg driven, all took off and swung their hats, and gave three cheers. And if the building were to be a meeting-house, the minister would be present, to add a prayer to the cheers.

The foregoing bees were attended only by men and boys. Females never took part in them, except, as was sometimes the case, to aid the man's wife to prepare a supper. They never took any part with the males in the labor. But women had their bees. When a woman had prepared her patchwork, her wadding, and arranged all into a suitable shape for a quilt, and put it all upon the quilting frame, she sent round invitations to all the young girls and younger married women, far and near, to come to the quilting at an appointed afternoon. They came, often several miles, on horseback, and through the woods. Then the quilting frame was laid on the tops of four chairs, one at each corner, and the women drew up and plied their needles, and kept at it till the quilt was made ready for the bed. All things were cleared away, and a supper of custards, nut-cakes, short-cake, and butter and cheese and tea, served up. The young men came in the evening, and then were music and dancing, and other amusements. These were called quilting bees; but were not often occasions of drunkenness.

The various bees fill a large place in the mental horizon of my childhood. They were household topics of conversation, around the table and the evening fire, and were of great interest to the indwellers of those forest homes. But they were sources of a vast amount of drunkenness; and while there were great outcryings against excessive drinking, not a word was ever uttered against the drinking custom. He would have been counted a fool or a madman, who should have declared all drinking, distilling, and vending of alcoholic liquor to be wrong and ruinous.

I believe there was scarce a family for miles around, in which some near and dear relative was not a drunkard. I have often heard it remarked as an extraordinary event, that there should be so many sons in my father's family, and not one of them a drunkard. Very many of my playmates have, years ago, gone down to the drunkard's grave, with whom I was very intimate, and who were very dear to me. They were kind, generous, loving and daring children of the forest; but they fell victims to the drinking custom, which was then sanctioned by universal consent. Tee-totalism would have saved them. But there were none to publish it.

It was a very common custom for the men in that forest region to chew or smoke tobacco, and the women often took it in snuff—and old women sometimes smoked. I have no recollection of ever seeing my father chew or smoke one particle of tobacco. No tobacco, no cigars, no snuff, no pipes, were kept in the house, in my childhood, except on one occasion. The taste and the smell of tobacco, or tobacco smoke, was then and has ever been disgusting to me, though I have smoked many a pipe and cigar since those days. Till from twelve to twenty-three years old, I never attempted to smoke tobacco.

My paternal grand-mother, in her extreme age, being eighty, followed her children from the older settlements of New England to the west, to spend her last days with them. She spent a winter with my father. I had never seen her before. I loved that kind old woman; and as it was my charge to prepare wood, make her fire, warm her room, and arrange it for her before she arose in the morning; to set her chair, to bring her water to wash and drink, and to go her errands, I became greatly fond of her, and attentive to her. She was my charge, and I watched over her with fond affection and reverence.

It was one part of my business to see that she was supplied with tobacco and a pipe, and to fill her pipe with tobacco, to light it and hand it to her. She was a great smoker, generally smoking several times in a day. Every thing about tobacco was disgusting. She used to tell me if I would only learn to smoke or chew, it would be more agreeable. This was, of course, true; but I did not then understand the full meaning of that truth. So one evening, when alone with her, under her direction, I undertook to learn to smoke. I filled the pipe, lighted it, and began to suck in and puff out the smoke. I soon began to feel sick, but my venerable instructress told me to persevere, and all would come right. I did, but the sickness increased. I grew so giddy, that I could not walk or stand or sit: the nausea was intolerable. I vomited; and after a while grew better, and crept to my bed, and arose nearly well next morning. But that cured me of smoking for the time being. I still helped my grandmother to her pipe as usual, but never joined her again. . . .

My grandmother removed to the home of another of her children in the forests of Pennsylvania, and there she died.

Scarce any objects of my childhood acquaintance come to my mind with fresher and deeper interest than the Indians, or Aborigines of America. The middle and western parts of New York State were covered with woods, in which were many Indians. No child of white, or professedly Christian parents was allowed to grow up in that region, without imbibing more or less hatred and horror of the Indians. Tales of Indian cruelties were in the mouths of all mothers and nurses. In the summer season, companies of Indians were often seen wandering over that region unmolested; hunting in the woods, fishing in the creeks, rivers, ponds and lakes; or going from house to house, selling neatly made baskets of bark or willow, variously painted, or moccasins of dressed deer skin, beautifully ornamented with beads of all colors, made of bones, or the shells of fish. These Indians used to show great dexterity in the use of the bow and arrow, and teach the boys how to make and use them.

I used to feel a deep interest in meeting these little parties of wandering Indians. Though I never heard about them, except in connection with scenes of massacres and murders, I never had any fear of them. So far as I saw them, they were as kind and trustworthy as other people. I have heard them state the wrongs, cruelties and murders perpetrated upon them by professedly Christian whites, and my sympathies were all with them. Their warriors were solemn, dignified men, with their fearful tomahawks and scalping knives; but every thing about them invested them with interest to me.

One little incident affected me deeply. My father and his family were at breakfast one bright summer morning. A party of Indians came along, some ten or twelve in number—men, women and children. They sat down on the ground, a little way from the door, which was open, allowing them to look in and see us at our morning meal. There they sat, waiting till we were done. After we had arisen from the table, a young girl entered, and asked if she, and her parents, and brothers and sisters, and the others, could have something to eat. My mother told her to wait awhile, and she would get a breakfast for them. Meat, potatoes, and bread were in due time set on; knives and forks and plates furnished, and chairs put round. They came in, sat down, and tried to use the knives and forks and plates; but they were awkward enough, and had great merriment over it, for one or two had cut their lips. My father told them to use their hands, and never mind their forks and knives. They did, and got on more to their satisfaction. They finished eating, and all arose, standing around the table, thanking my father and mother for their kindness.

When I was but ten or twelve years old, I thought, and still think, that professedly civilized and Christian whites have been far more revengeful, unjust and murderous to the Indians of America, than those Indians have been to them.

I was endowed with a physical hardihood and capability of endurance that knew no fatigue, and could meet any amount of physical privation or exposure without fear or shrinking. I had a self-possession and presence of mind in sudden excitements and dangers; a fearless confidence in myself to do whatever I attempted; a power of concentrating my thoughts, and feelings, and energies, on a given object, combined with a steady perseverance in doing whatever I undertook to do, which never was discouraged; and these things would have made me a desperado, had the profession of arms been my portion. I have often felt that I should have been a fearful besom of destruction, had I been left to the gratification of my desires after military glory.

My father was a Federalist, and sided with England in the wars of Napoleon. My oldest brother, who had charge of the farm, and most all things at home, while my father was away building houses, was a Democrat, and sided with Napoleon. They often held discussions over Napoleon's progress. It has often been cause for wonder to me, with what absorbing interest I used to hear and read of that man's movements; for though a child, my heart always triumphed in his victories, his rapid movements, his sudden encounters with the combined armies of all Europe. It was the fearful daring and energy of the man that kindled up my young heart. Many a stirring speech have I made, in the dreams of my childhood, to an army, to animate them to battle and to victory.

Stories and histories about wars and warriors were then my meat and drink. The conquests and wars of Cortez and Pizarro, in Mexico and Peru; the wars between the Puritans and the Indians, and the events of the Revolutionary War, were familiar to my mind, and deeply engraven on my heart. The Jewish wars and massacres were the portions of the Bible most familiar and interesting to my mind. Many an hour and day have I spent, in secret and stillness, in the house, in the barn, and in the woods, poring over those scenes of violence and blood, till the very soul of war seemed to be breathed into me. The martial music, the fife, and drum, and bugle horn; the motion, the order, the firm and measured tread; the glittering of swords, and the roar of musketry and cannon, on military parade days, were invested with enchantment to me.

In early life, I got hold of an old military catechism,

that aimed to teach the science and mysteries of war; of drilling and disciplining armies; of the sword and the gun exercise; of shooting and stabbing men, and of arranging and ordering battles; and over this book I pored till it was as familiar to me as my alphabet. . . .

III

I have done with the child; now for the youth. But before entering upon this period, I would remark that my mind has, ever since childhood, been struggling to cast out many of my early impressions, as deadly enemies to its advancement in purity and enjoyment, as the bodily system seeks to cast out a fever or a plague; the former being no less certain elements of death to the soul than the latter are to the body. . . .

Physical strength and health were my father's first aim in our education; and in this plan he succeeded admirably with us all. When about fourteen, I first began to study Arithmetic. The first step in this process was, to learn the multiplication table. This being a mere effort of memory, was quickly despatched; for this faculty had been thoroughly developed and strengthened in learning to spell and read. No one can tell the ecstacy I felt as I came to understand the fundamental principles of Arithmetic. No miser ever gloated over his gold as I have contemplated propositions which I had demonstrated. When I saw, by the figures on my slate, that the result could not be otherwise, I have shouted for joy, to feel that I had found that about which there could be no perplexing uncertainty. All was light; my mind seemed to settle down upon a certain, immutable basis. Such had been my training, up to that period of my life, that a kind of painful uncertainty seemed to hang over me, and every thing around me. It was the study of Arithmetic that made me feel that there was a fixed and indisputable truth and reality in my existence. I loved those demonstrations; and when a proposition was put on my slate for me to work out, and I had gone through, step by step, and understood the reason of every one, till I knew, for certainty, that the demonstration was complete, I used to feel unmingled satisfaction in writing the whole down in a book which I had for the purpose, before I rubbed the figures from my slate. My fondness for Arithmetic knew no moderation. My dormant mental powers sprang into life with an energy and joyousness of which I had hitherto no conception. I knew not that I had any such powers, and was capable of any such enjoyments. I knew that I had intense physical energy, and that I sometimes became wild with joy in putting it forth; but this was a feeling of pleasure more intense and more absorbing, and in gratifying it, I could sit motionless for hours. My restless physical nature became suddenly quiet under the influence of this absorbing feeling. My slate and my Arithmetic were scarce ever out of my hands, from my entrance into school in the morning, to my departure from it at night. . . .

For three or four winters did I go to school for about ten weeks each winter, and worked on the farm with my brothers in summer. The summer was a season of activity and development to my body; the winter, a season of growth to my mind.

Spelling, Reading, Writing, Arithmetic—these constituted the sum total of my school studies, during childhood and youth. I never studied one lesson in Grammar, Geography, History, Political Economy, or physical, intellectual or moral Philosophy. Not an effort was made to teach me how to express my thoughts or feelings in writing; a defect in my early training which I have ever had reason to deplore. . . . Only by the study of Arithmetic did the school ever do any thing to develop and strengthen any of my intellectual powers, except my memory.

When quite young, there was a total eclipse of the sun in June. That event made a deep impression on me. I heard much about it for weeks beforehand. I knew not what it was to be like, except that it was to be dark about mid-day. I was hoeing Indian corn, with two older brothers. They sent me off on an errand, and as I passed to the place, I could see the woods begin to look dingy. I started to return, and by this time, birds and beasts began to be in extraordinary excitement, rushing to the roost and the lair. The woods became dark and gloomy. I was in the midst, and night seemed to drop down upon the scene in the midst of daylight. The forest had the same gloomy appearance which it had at night. The sun had an appearance I never saw before; it seemed to be in a process of going out, till, for a moment, it was all gone. I knew where I was, and the way out of the wood, and what was the matter, and had no fear. I stood still in the woods, and contemplated the scene with wonder. It soon passed, and I went on my way; but an awe was on my spirit long afterwards, whenever I saw the heavens by day or night.

My step-mother died in the winter of 1814. I was seventeen years old. Once more it brought death very near to me. I felt that there was a vacancy in the family. A familiar object was wanting. I had contracted a feeling of strong affection for her. After her death, my feelings towards my half-sisters, who were bereft of their mother, became very strong. They were all small, and they appeared very desolate. My heart felt for them far more than for any loss I had sustained. Now, more than ever, I loved to be with them, and to try to amuse them. . . .

The spring after my step-mother died, I left the house of my childhood and youth, to learn the hat-making business. My father considered habits of industry and economy the richest legacy he could leave to his children; one that could not but be useful to them, whatever might be their station and condition in life. I do not believe that one of them ever regretted his training in this particular.

In April, 1814, my father went with me on horseback to the village of Norwich, in the county of Chenango, about thirty miles west of Hartwick. There he left me with David G. Bright. I had no particularly unhappy feelings about leaving home. I knew not what this meant. I had never been from home to spend more than one day at a time. Nor had I any very desolate feelings, when my father left me to return home; but he seemed to feel the separation keenly. He left me, bidding me good bye, with a tearful eye and a sad countenance. But he departed, riding one horse, and leading the one on which I had rode. Then began a new existence for me. I had left the paternal roof, and was afloat in the world.

I had made up my mind that I would learn thoroughly how to make hats, that I would submit to all necessary hardships to perfect myself in it. There were several journeymen and apprentices in the shop. I was the youngest apprentice, and, according to rules in such case made and provided, had to make the fires and to fill the kettles in the morning, and to keep the fires going, and the kettles filled and boiling all day; to pack away wool and furs; to chop wool, and cut fur from the pelts; to boil glue; to set hats out to dry by day, and bring them in at night; to sweep the floor, clean out the ashes, and to keep the shop tidy. I knew that, if I would ever be a hatter, who would not be ashamed of his work or shop, I must learn to do all these things. I set myself cheerfully and heartily to do them, and I gave satisfaction to all. At the same time, I began to apply my hand to the operation of bowing, setting up, planking, blocking and dying hats. In a few weeks I understood what was to be done in each step of the process, and before the term of my trial was out, I could take the raw material and make a hat without aid from any one. I felt great pride in being able to do this, and contemplated my first hat with no small delight, rude though it was.

I was put on trial for three months; at the end of which, if David G. Bright, or Boss, as he was called, or myself, wished the connection to cease, it was to cease. But at the end of that time, my father came again, and both parties being agreed, indentures were drawn and signed between my father and Mr. Bright, binding me an apprentice to him for the term of four years, or till I was twenty-one.

But what had been my experience, in my inner man, during these three months? Of my sufferings, and the shock to my moral feelings, and my loathing and disgust at certain things, my father knew nothing till long afterwards. Had he known the moral crucifixion which my feelings passed through daily and almost hourly, I believe he would have cut his right hand off before he would have let me remain there.

I was home-sick, without one moment's cessation, after the first few days, except when asleep. There is a feeling of wretchedness, the like of which I never felt before nor since; such a sinking of spirit; such loneliness; such a longing for human sympathy, and such a fear, lest any one should know how I felt, and be able to sympathise with me; such a loathing of food, and dread of not seeming to relish it; such an utter distaste for amusement, and such a fear of being thought not to enjoy it; such a prostration of soul and body, and yet such an effort to appear cheerful and energetic; all this, lest the real state of my feelings should be discovered, and I should be subjected to the laughter of those around me. Those three months were an age of torment to me, by reason of my home-sickness.

I found my local attachments and home affections were intense and enduring. I knew nothing about myself in these particulars, till taught by these three months' experience. I knew not how I loved my father, my elder brothers and sisters; I knew not how dear to me was the younger brother, whose spirit I had so often and so cruelly vexed; nor had I any conception of my affection for my three little half-sisters. Every remembered instance of disobedience to my father; of cruel vexation of my younger brother; or of want of attention to any of my brothers and sisters; all rose up before me, and, seen through the magnifying glass of my home-sickness, appeared to me like heinous crimes that never ought to be forgiven. I was very desolate and wretched; and many times have I walked alone at night, in some woods, near the shop, and sat on the border of the Chenango river, which flowed about three-fourths of a mile from the house, and there wept for very sickness of heart, longing for the home of my childhood. But, during this time, I had to attend to my daily work, and to conceal my feelings in my own bosom; knowing, that an exhibition of them before my shop-mates would only excite their scorn, or their coarse and brutal jests. . . .

But I had other sources of misery; and sources which had caused my father and family far more anxiety, had they known of their existence.

Three times a day, and every day, during those three months, I went to a whiskey shop to get whiskey for the journeymen. There was not a day, rain or shine, foul or fair, holy days, or unholy days, in which I did not repair with a bottle to a shop about twenty rods off, to get whiskey. Not a night came, which did not find some of these journeymen more or less drunk. In this state, their profanity, their obscenity, their utter brutishness, knew no bounds. They earned much money, but spent it on strong drinks, and I had to be a purveyor to their filthiness and corruption.

I rebelled somewhat against this at first, for I had an undefined feeling, even then, that it was wrong thus to administer to their drunkenness. But I was told that it was a part of the youngest apprentice's business to fetch whiskey to the journeymen. I submitted, but with no ease or heartiness of mind. . . . Though often urged to drink, I do not remember that I ever tasted one drop of whiskey, or of any other intoxicating liquor in that shop. The drinking and the accompaniments, and my constant hastening to and from the vile drunkery for whiskey, disgusted me with the very sight of the foul stuff, and settled me in my determination not to drink with them, come what might. This resolve I kept, and it saved my father's son from the drunkard's grave. What helped to confirm me in this resolution was, the remark of my brother Chester, as I bid him adieu on leaving home: "Henry, I'd rather see you in a felon's dungeon, than to see you a drunkard." That was a timely warning, though he knew not the great need of it at the time.

In progress of time, I became master of every step in the process of making all kinds of hats from wool and fur: the use of silk for making hats was not then thought of in that region. I felt real satisfaction in being able to make a hat, because I loved to contemplate the work when finished, and because I felt a pleasure in carrying it through the various stages. The process of manufacturing hats out of wool or fur is one which no man, who has a taste for skilful works of the hand, can contemplate without interest. Making a fur hat is a light, tasteful and fairy-like operation, in some of the stages; one requiring close attention, and light and skilful hands. And when the hat is finished, nothing can be more soft and delicate. The fur of the beaver, or of the otter, is susceptible of a very soft, bright and high finish. . . .

In about one year after I entered the shop, I became the

oldest apprentice. We were gathered from widely different and distant quarters; but having, for the most part, been all born and brought up as children of the forest, we were all familiar with the same objects, and accustomed to the same hardy, active life. But we differed widely as possible in our early religious training, and in our tempers.

I have often looked back with wonder upon that group of young lads, just springing into manhood, with our discordant tempers and dispositions, and admired how we contrived to live so lovingly together. Our varied and joyous spirits, with now and then an outbreak, were all so controlled and blended as to produce a kind, generous and happy company. On no part of my life do I look back with more satisfaction than on my brief but pleasant connection with those apprentices; and I have often regarded with surprise the steady and redeeming influence which we had on one another: I acted out my peculiarities of mind and disposition; they did the same; yet they came to love and respect me greatly, as I did them, and our parting, when it came, was a sad one. I made it a rule, from which I never deviated with those lads (with one exception) never to fret and scold at them, or to tease them. I had learned a lesson, never more to be forgotten, from the deep sorrow I felt at having vexed and tormented the generous spirit of my younger brother. Say or do what they would to me personally, I never complained of them. When any thing was done by them, of which I had to bear the blame, or expose them, I always bore the blame; if any thing extraordinary was to be done, that required increased effort, I never put these extra tasks on them, nor asked them to assist me, if I could do them alone. If I wished for any tool, to carry on my work or to administer to my necessities or comfort, I never asked one of those apprentices to hand it to me; I never called on them to do

any thing for me which I could do for myself; and this I
carried out while I was with them, and this habit of waiting on myself not only gave me a standing with them, but
it also strengthened in me a feeling and habit of self-
reliance and personal independence which has been invaluable to me in the life I have been called to live the
last twenty years.

To one practice I invariably adhered with these apprentices. If I had apples, plums, pears, melons, or any
good edible, whether given to me or bought with my own
money, I gave them a portion. This was my uniform conduct towards those generous-hearted lads. I had no enjoyments in which they did not share, if it were possible for
me to extend it to them. . . . But in another point of view,
I have ever regarded my conduct with far less satisfaction; though at the time I considered it right and expedi-
ent. I never received from them the least thing. I never
asked them to share any thing they had with me; and
when it was offered, I never received it. But did they
offer? They never failed; and those generous boys often
felt hurt because I would not receive from them whatever
token of affection and regard they had to give; and they
ever laid their apple, their roast potato, their bunch of
raisins, or other tokens of kindness, by my place of work,
in my desk, in my pocket, or by my bed, that I might take
it without knowing from whom it came; but it was immediately returned to any of them who would take it; and if
all refused it, it was put aside and left to be disposed of by
chance. They always received of mine; I never received of
theirs, but always gave a peremptory and determined re-
fusal to their proffered kindness.

I was wrong, entirely wrong; I did not do as I would be
done by; for, had those boys refused my offers as I did
theirs, it would have vexed me sorely, and deprived me of
a source of one of my greatest luxuries at that time. They

often told me I was wrong; and that I did not do by them as I wished them to do by me. . . .

I determined that I would never be betrayed into an outbreak of anger towards those young lads; I have no recollection that I ever was. Whatever of anger I might feel, I kept it to myself; and never did I speak to them when I was excited, except in a deliberate, cool tone and manner. So disciplining myself, and that in proportion as I was soured in spirit, I became cool and deliberate in outward speech and demeanor. I then acquired a calmness of voice, and a coolness and self-possession of manners, that have stood me in stead since, in many a stern encounter with men of violence and blood. It has been of infinite service to me in public debates, on Anti-Slavery and Non-Resistance.

My fondness for music still continued. My shrill fife or soft flute often beguiled my moments of leisure. A singing school was taught in the village one winter. I greatly enjoyed attending it. The school was taught by a man who was counted very religious, and he always opened and closed his singing by a prayer. He was much given to talking to people about their souls, and about being converted. But he was a sweet singer, and for this, and this only, I attended. I used to carry my flute, and play on that; he had a harp, which he played. He would often try to get a word with me about my soul, but I contrived to shun these talks, while I reaped the pleasure and benefit of his musical powers, which were far more agreeable and profitable to me than his skill in talking about conversion and the state of the soul.

For several weeks after he left, I conducted the singing school, meeting some fifty persons every Sunday evening, and instructing them in singing. This I enjoyed greatly. Teaching this singing school had a powerful effect on my own feelings and conduct. Mine was a gratuitous school, and I taught it merely for the pleasure it afforded me. Mr. Bright had bought and presented to me a fine flute, and this helped me on greatly. Then, whenever I went to meeting, I led the singing; and I often went solely to do this, for I had no pleasure or profit in the preaching or praying. But the church members got into a discussion whether it was right for any one to sing in meeting who was not converted, and had not joined the church, and I gave it up. I felt that it was right for me to sing in the woods or fields, under the open canopy of heaven, in the presence of all created and uncreated beings, and I could not see how it could be wrong for me to sing in a meeting-house, to a few Presbyterians.

We were never controlled, in the least, by the man with whom we lived, as to our manner of spending the Sabbath. Whether we went to meeting or staid at home; whether we read the Bible or read a newspaper; whether we were asleep or awake, in the house or in the fields, merry or sad, he cared not, provided we had put off our soiled clothes, washed, and put on clean ones, and did not disturb the neighbors, nor get into mischief. I often strolled away, quietly and alone, down by the Chenango —a beautiful river, and flowing through the sweet valley in which the village of Norwich stood. In the meadows on its banks, have I spent many Sabbaths, under large apple trees, scattered here and there, that were planted by the Indians. Sometimes others of the young lads were with me, and we bathed in the clear river, and were refreshed. We picked berries, ate apples (no one questioning our right to eat what apples we wanted) laughed, sang, and inhaled the sweet, pure air of heaven, after a week's work in the shop.

In about eighteen months after entering the shop, I would do my day's work by the middle of the afternoon. Then I used to put away my work, wash, and go to my room, and read or study. I obtained an old English Grammar, and made myself master of it; and afterwards, when I came to study the philosophy of language, I found I had all the essential principles in my mind—first introduced there in my little garret where I slept, and after I had accomplished my daily task at making hats.

Geography, too, was there first studied by me. I became acquainted with the elementary principles of this science; and my mind, after being employed in shaping wool and fur into an article for the comfort and use of man, grappled with oceans and continents, mountains and rivers, states and empires. I had a very large and minute Geography of the Western Hemisphere, and became most familiar with its climates, mountains, rivers, lakes and bays. The enlargement of my mind by this study was an inexhaustible fountain of profit and pleasure to me.

Of Astronomy, too, I obtained some knowledge. After spending most of the day with my mind engaged in business avocations, I would retire to my sleeping garret, and there, coat off, and sleeves rolled up, I would mount to the heavens, and wander and revel among the planets, and explore the mysteries of the vaulted sky. This was to me unspeakable bliss. I used to feel a sense of overwhelming grandeur, as I pursued the study of Astronomy. I had no means to go far into it; but what I did study gave me a taste for it which I afterwards gratified to the full.

History I read, too. I borrowed Rollin's *Ancient History*, and read it through. Mr. Bright, seeing me so fond of reading history, bought me a very fine edition, and gave it to me. I then read it through again, till its leading military characters and events were familiar to me. I obtained a history of the early settlement of the Puritans in New England, and of their wars with the Indians, and this I devoured. But even then, my heart and head took the part of the Indians against the Puritans. These were my principal studies and readings during my apprenticeship. Arithmetic I never gave up. On this study, my mind rested as on nothing else. Over all other things there was doubt, uncertainty; here all was light, demonstration, and nothing to be gainsayed or doubted.

One of our fellow apprentices, named Henry Folsom, was a strange mixture. He was the only son of his mother, who was a widow, and who fondly doted on him, as her solace and support. He was the oldest apprentice in years, and the youngest in apprenticeship. He was taken into the shop at the earnest request of his kind mother, rather to acquire habits of application to some active and useful employment, than from any necessity—she having enough to sustain him without labor. Poor Henry! He was the daily and hourly victim of some practical joke; and then came down upon us the storms of his wrath; for when thus run upon, he seldom discriminated, but considered us all as leagued against him.

Scarcely had he entered the shop, before his sensitiveness to jokes was made manifest. His great foible was seized upon as a source of amusement, and he was subjected to a fiery ordeal. He often inflicted personal injuries upon his tormentors; but the spirit which tormented him was one which never leads to the infliction of injuries upon the body, and which leads men to suffer great bodily pain without retaliation. It was the spirit of fun and frolic, and not of ill-will or hatred; though the miseries it inflicts, the vexations and goadings of spirit, and the mental torments, are often more difficult to endure patiently than any bodily sufferings. It was so with that lad. Poor fellow! he used to often come to me with tears of vexation, completely worn down by the continual ridicule to which he was subjected, and beseech me to help him. I have often procured him a respite for a few days, but it was of no use; his awkwardness was irresistibly ludicrous, and the spirit of fun would not be controlled.

He never could learn to shape wool or fur into a decent or useful hat; he would always "bungle" some where in the process, and after spoiling many a pound of wool, and being the laughing-stock of the shop for about one year, he was sent home to his mother, where his spirit found repose, after being sorely tempest-tossed. . . .

I cannot but allude here to my early feelings towards those who are deformed in body or mind, or are laboring under any disabilities of person or position. My father impressed on my mind, in childhood, the exceeding cruelty and wickedness of making the personal deformity of any human being a subject of merriment; and I never could, with any satisfaction, ridicule, or hear others ridicule such persons, either to their faces or behind their backs. I had no sympathy with it. When a child and a youth, I never could bear to hear ragged people, or beggars, or the lame, halt, blind, or deaf, made subjects of mirth among children. The same feeling I had about idiotic and insane people. It ever seemed to me indicative of a mean, coarse and cruel disposition in children, to make game of such persons. People naturally deformed in body or mind, should ever be treated kindly; it is aggravating their burdens to make them objects of merriment. Such ought to be made to feel and know that they always have our sympathies, and that we delight to help bear their burdens, and make them forget their infirmities. This would soothe and comfort them, and strew their otherwise sad pathway with flowers. I have ever felt it to be utterly wrong to mock at any human being for any thing about him he could not help, and in which he had no choice.

The same feeling in me extended to drunkards. I never

could have any enjoyment or merriment over the babblings and staggerings of a drunkard; and when I used to
see children making fun of them, and vexing them, I ever
felt an inclination to take their part, and save them from
their youthful tormentors.

One of our fellow-apprentices was born out of wedlock.
He had a mother, who had trained him up in a good way,
and whom he dearly loved; but he never knew a father,
nor was known by one. This was one of the best tempered,
most steady, intelligent and enterprising lads in the shop.
He was generally beloved by the rest, and by the whole
family. He was generous, and kind to all. But I have heard
that youth reproached, because he was born contrary to
law. They made him suffer for the fault of his parents. I
never could see the justice of that public sentiment, that
meets [*sic*] out reproach to such people on account of the
circumstances of their birth. It seems to me no less unnat-
ural and monstrous, than unjust and cruel. I never could
hear that generous shopmate mocked on this account,
without a feeling of indignation; and I felt then, and do
still feel, that my indignation was a just and righteous
one. . . .

Mrs. Bright was a truly good woman, her religion being
a principle of daily life, governing her feelings and her
practice. An old woman, by the name of Snow, used to
visit her. She was a kind of mother to all in the pretty
village, having seen it spring up amid the wilderness; herself being one of the first settlers. She knew every body,
and every body knew and loved her. She could tell the
history of the past, when few beside Indians dwelt on the
borders of the Chenango river, and fished in its waters. I
used to love to meet that kind Christian woman, and hear
her talk. I became well acquainted with her. She used to
ask permission for me to come into the house, that she
might talk with me; and, as much as I dreaded to have

others talk to me about my soul, I was ever glad to hear her talk about any thing. She spoke so kindly, so sweetly, and so cheerfully, that it was pleasant to hear her. There was no awful, holy manner, tone or look, about her; no affectation, no solemn grimace, no making up religious faces at me; but she just entered into my feelings and answered my questions, kindly and naturally, without any solemn and ominous shake of the head. She had much to say about the Bible; and though I had been taught to believe every chapter and verse of it to be the word of God, yet I used to ask her, "How she knew it was?" Her only answer was: "I know it is, for I *feel* that it is." When I asked her how she knew there was a God and another state of existence, her ever ready and ever positive and only answer was: "I know there is a future state and a God, because I am conscious of it." When I used to tell her that her feelings could be no evidence to me, she would ask me, "Do you not feel the same evidence that there is a God and a future state, that you have of your own present existence? I do," she would say, "and can no more doubt the one than the other." To this argument, I could never find an answer. That kindly and truly Christian woman taught me many good things. She would insist that her consciousness was sufficient evidence to her of the truth and power of Christianity; and that if ever I felt that truth and power, then my feelings would become evidence to me.

But I would never allow the authority of the church and ministers in settling truth, at which she was greatly grieved. She used to urge me to read for myself the Bible, which I promised on one occasion to do from beginning to end. Had I always, from childhood, been spoken to in this frank and kindly way on religious matters, as they were called, I believe my whole life had been a happier one. I should have had less to contend with. My acquaintance

with her is a kind of bright sunny spot in my mental horizon, so far as my mind has been exercised on points of
theology. She directed me in fact to religion, as a living
principle in the soul—to God as an ever present, ever
controlling Guide to my youth—taught me to look to Him
as a little child to a father. The spirit, embodied in that
woman, seemed inexpressibly lovely to me; and I could
not but wish that it might be mine.

I had been in that shop about five months, when I was
allowed two weeks' absence to visit my father. During
that whole time, I had not ceased to pine in my heart for
home. Those few months taught me to know the full im-
port of the "home of childhood." It was a moment of joyous impatience, when, at the dawn of day, and before any
one was stirring, I started for home. It was about thirty
miles, and nearly half the distance lay through woods,
with here and there a clearing, and scarcely an apology
for a road. I could not wait for breakfast, and I was to
walk the distance in an intensely hot August day, and the
little springs and brooks were dried up.

I took some pieces of dried salt fish in my pocket and
started, and soon struck into the woods, and came across
one range of hills after another, until I became ravenously
hungry. I ate my salt fish—then came the thirst, not less
intolerable than the hunger; and I could find no spring or
brook to slake it. To add to my troubles, a new pair of
boots pinched and blistered my feet. Off went the boots
and stockings, and carrying them in my hand, I walked
barefoot the rest of the way, being some fourteen miles.
As I came down upon the Butternut Creek, I entered a little
dirty tavern. I asked, "Have you any beer?" "I have," said
the landlord. "Let me have a pint," said I—my mind
thinking all the while only of beer made of ginger, and
various kinds of pleasant roots. He soon presented the
beer. It frothed on the top, and looked as if it would taste

deliciously. I put it to my mouth, nor stopped to breathe, till it was all down. And this was my first drink of ale or porter, and the last. I have no recollection of having drank one drop from that day to this. That was enough to last one man a life-time. Besides the bitterness of it, which was insupportable, the foul stuff so affected me that I could not walk with comfort for two hours.

I reached the top of the mountain whence I could look down upon the sweet home of my childhood, long before night. There I sat down, and for an hour feasted my spirit by looking upon the dear spot. The hills, the forests, the brooks, and all, were the same. I hastened down to my father's house, and there were my father, my brothers, and my three young sisters, and, also, my father's third wife, ready to welcome me. I found a second step-mother, and my father seemed perfectly happy in the marriage. Every body and every thing seemed glad to see me back again.

Here, with what interest did I visit every meadow, pasture and field, where I had worked, and where I had watched after the sheep and cows and horses, and every corner where I had picked raspberries, blackberries, strawberries, wild cherries, plums and gooseberries, and wandered through the woods and by the streams, where I had so often sported. For a time, my heart was full. Home was associated with the place, as well as with father, brothers and sisters. This feeling of home, as a locality, is nearly gone; and now I feel that where duty is, there is home. I often feel that the universe is the beautiful, magnificent, illimitable home of my spirit. Still, even now, I love to visit that sweet little vale.

I staid one fortnight in the indulgence of my domestic affections; then departed again on foot for my distant place of residence. An older brother accompanied me a few miles to the top of the hill that looked down upon the home valley, and there we parted in the woods; he returned, and I went about half a mile deeper into the woods, and there sat down on a log, took out my flageolet, and played a sweet, plaintive air to relieve my desolation.

But a change had come over me during my five months' absence. I had come to think and act more for myself on all matters; and I felt that I was in the right way. I came to the hat-shop again; went to work with a better relish, and I have never felt that dreadful feeling of homesickness since.

I come now to an important period, in which an event occurred that changed the whole course of my life. I was at this time twenty years of age. It took place in the winter of 1817.

A Presbyterian church had been organized in the village. Having no minister to do their work, they used to do their own singing, and praying, and preaching. Rev. John Truair, of Sherburne—a village twelve miles north of Norwich—was invited to spend a few weeks among them, as an evangelist. He was an extraordinary man; middle-aged, tall and erect, with piercing black eyes; foppish in his dress and manners, and having a habit of playing with his watch key and seal, while preaching or praying. He was a man of stern brow, emphatic and determined tone of voice, and thoroughly versed in the art of moving the feelings, and producing an excitement in society.

This man came; began to hold meetings; to sing, pray, and preach; to go from house to house, visiting families, talking to every individual about his or her soul, and praying with them. Soon rumor said that a revival had begun. The minister assured the people who flocked to hear his eloquence, "that the Lord was about to visit that village, and to gather into His fold His elect." This announcement had a startling effect, and led to the inquiry among many —"Who are the elect?" And many made up their minds to be among the chosen ones. Meetings were multiplied; praying and singing were more frequent and energetic; exhortations and appeals to the unconverted were more earnest. Soon it was rumored about that this one and that one were "under distress of mind," and people were asked in public to pray for them. Notes were presented by individuals to the minister, asking him and the church to pray for an unconverted relative or friend. These notes were read and commented on by the minister, and all were urged to put up prayers for such persons. Prayer and conference meetings, and family visitations, were multiplied. The excitement soon extended through the village and surrounding neighborhoods. There was not a family nor an individual that was not more or less moved by that excitement, to approve or oppose. Converts soon began to appear. It was made public that such and such persons had "found or experienced religion." It was expected that those who had been "brought out" would at once bear witness to the fact, by rising up in a prayer or conference meeting, tell their experience, make an exhortation to their old companions, telling them they could go no more with them—that they had "chosen a portion among the people of God."

From the first arrival of John Truair in the town, I had been greatly taken with the man, though I had not formed any personal acquaintance with him, nor did I wish to do it. I admired his preaching and praying in public, but I had not a willingness to have him talk to me about my soul, or to have it supposed that I felt any concern about religion. Yet I was spell-bound by his preaching and praying, before I had a thought of applying what he said to my own case.

In his crowded meetings, in the evenings, in private dwellings, or in school-houses, I used to get behind all others in some dark corner, where none could be witness to my interest; and there I would sit, completely fascinated, as I heard that man pour forth his prayers and preachings. I often felt overcome by them, but concealed my emotion, lest I should be thought to be "under distress of mind."

I conducted the singing in these meetings when I was present. This I greatly enjoyed. Most rousing hymns were given out, and I used to sing them in the most exciting tunes; so that the effect of the singing was not much less on the people assembled, than the preaching and praying. The revival had come down upon the whole village, and was sweeping over it like a whirlwind. Nothing else was talked of. All amusements among the young people were abandoned, and the whole village flocked to the exciting scenes of the prayer and conference meetings.

I certainly partook of that excitement in no ordinary degree. I thoroughly enjoyed it; and yet there were times when it was not all enjoyment. The man must have been of more than Indian hardihood and self-possession not to have been excited. But at the first, it was my enjoyment in seeing a whole community thoroughly aroused; in seeing them look, speak and act in earnest, as if urged forward by some irresistible impulse to the accomplishment of some great end; this, together with the energetic and determined manner and eloquence of the minister, was the sole cause of my deep interest in the revival. I could not have made merry with that scene; I did not wish to have it cease; the whole town was in terrible earnest, in pursuit of something which they deemed worthy to call forth their mightiest energies. Beneath all my enjoyment, I felt that I had never been "under distress of mind," and been "brought out," and that I must be. I certainly felt, and at times, when alone, painfully felt, that I must seek and find that thing called religion, or I must suffer the torments of hell for ever. This was impressed upon my mind at times with great force, in my private moments. I finally gave myself up to this feeling entirely.

It was under this deeply excited state of mind, this determination to "seek religion and to find it," that I began to read the Bible with a view to read it through, and judge for myself of its contents. I was enabled so to manage my work in the shop, as to have several hours every day, and all Sunday, for reading. I had a Bible, in which my father had written his own name and mine, and which he had given me when I left home. This I began to read with a purpose to go through the whole of it. I read on, verse after verse and chapter after chapter, from the first to the last, and generally with a deepening interest, and a more settled purpose to make myself possessor of that hidden, but invaluable jewel which was called religion, and of which I had heard so much from my earliest childhood. The impression became daily more vivid, that I had not yet found religion, and that I must find it, and that this was the time to finish the work. I had begun it, and I felt as determined to go through with it, and finish what seemed to me to be the necessary work of conviction and conversion, as I ever was to learn a lesson, or to demonstrate a mathematical problem.

No pen could portray the anguish with which, at that time, I contemplated the fall of Adam and Eve. I had been thoroughly taught in the Westminster Catechism, and the questions and answers about the fall rose up to my excited mind with terrible distinctness. . . . I did then believe, as I sat in my little garret, on my rude old chest, reading the third chapter of Genesis, that when Adam ate the apple, I "sinned in him, and fell with him"; that, by that one act of Adam, I was "brought into a state of sin," was born destitute "of original righteousness," had received "corruption in my whole nature," had "lost all communion with God," "was under his wrath and curse," "made liable to all the miseries in this life, to death itself, and to the pains of hell forever."

I had a profound conviction of the understanding that all this was true, and, by turns, I scorned Adam with indignation, and then wept over his weakness and his fall. I bewailed my misfortune, for such I considered my existence to be under such circumstances, and wondered how my parents could dare to cause me to be, when they believed my being must, of necessity, be "under the wrath and curse of God." As I read through the New Testament, I felt that it must be true, and I longed to be possessed of its glorious spirit. What was the result of my reading? What did I find? I did not find religion.

The excitement went on, rather increasing than diminishing. Several of the leading men and women of the village had been convicted and converted. The conversion of a sedate, influential lawyer was announced. I was at the meeting when he first made known the fact, and gave a most stirring exhortation. This "brought out" others under distress of mind. I certainly was laboring under much anguish of mind; my enjoyment of the excitement still continued, but mingled with it was an abiding sense of wretchedness. The very operation of which I had so often thought and heard with dread, had commenced with me, and I felt myself going through it, in all its bitterness. I can say with truth, that but a small part of my distress had any reference to any particular act of wickedness which I had perpetrated. My anguish was the result of my theological belief, rather than of conscious wrong-feeling or doing. I was in a distracted state. My heart was at war with my head. My theology said I was "under the wrath and curse of God." My heart said No to that. My head said, I had "lost all communion with God." My heart said that I loved to be close to Him, and to feel that I lived and moved in Him. Thus was I sorely distressed; my heart an

utter infidel to my head, and my affections pouring con-
tempt upon my theology. Bitterly now did I suffer the
consequences of having imbibed, in childhood, a theology
at variance with the facts relating to my physical and
moral being. . . .

After being several weeks under this distress of mind, at
length I "was brought out." I had sought religion, and I
had found it, as I supposed, and as others did. I had always been taught to believe that persons would generally
know the exact time and place of their conversion. I had
often heard this point warmly debated, and many main-
tained that if the certain time and place were not known,
and could not be specified, this of itself was enough to
render null and void all other evidences of a change. The
first question to new converts often was: "Do you remember the time and place in which you were converted?" Of
course, this became an important point. I suppose I knew
the time and place at which the operation was wrought
upon me. I was in my little chamber, on my bed, reading and thinking over my calamitous state; ready, at
times, to curse the day that gave me birth under such
circumstances, and then ready to curse myself for thus
cursing that day. . . .

At length, as I thus lay brooding over my condition,
there was an instantaneous revolution in my feelings;
from deep anguish, I passed to great joy. There was a
sudden revulsion from sorrow to joy. I had found deliverance, and said to myself, "This is religion! I have found it
at last!"

I did then and long afterwards think I was then and
there made a Christian by that operation. It was this
sudden revulsion in my feelings, which I supposed constituted me a Christian. My distress about my unfortunate
and miserable condition as a descendant of Adam, and an
heir of his guilt and shame, was gone. I believed the doc-

trine still, but it did not greatly distress me. My indignation against Adam and my parents was gone, though I still
believed that they were very weak, for doing what they
knew involved such fearful consequences. A few evenings
after my "being brought out," there was to be a church-
meeting; where it was expected many would tell their
experience. Multitudes were there to hear. Among others,
I came upon the stand, and, to use the language which all
used, related "what the Lord had done to my soul"—a
phrase expressive simply of the process of being "under
distress of mind," and of "being brought out." So I told the
process through which I had passed.

The process, as I now think, was simply a mental one. I
did not suppose that "my deliverance" was designed to
suppress any wrong feelings, and to strengthen those that
are good; nor was I conscious of having been delivered
from any evil passion and habit. The deliverance which I
sought and found was one from darkness to light—from
sorrow to joy. I believe this was the impression of that
whole community respecting the religion which was to be
sought and found. It consisted in being punctual to attend
meetings; fearless and faithful to talk to persons about
their souls, and to warn them to escape from wrath to
come; faithful to keep the Sabbath, to join a church and
abide by its regulations, and to observe the sacrament. It
is certain that, in the estimation of the new converts, their
change referred mainly or wholly to such matters. This
the final event showed beyond contradiction.

Several young men in the place were determined to
arrest the excitement. To this end, they set on foot a ball.
They made great efforts; bespoke the best hall in the
place, engaged a famous musician to do the fiddling, issued their cards, prepared for their supper, and intended
to have a splendid dance. The evening came, and the
fiddler; but there were few dancers, male or female. There

had been a powerful excitement about the ball among those who sympathized with the revival. Their zeal became bolder and more intense than ever. The minister gave one of his most terrible sermons against it, as an atheistical design, as he expressed it, to "drive the Lord away from Norwich." A meeting was appointed the evening of the ball, and near where it was to be, in order that those who chose might have an opportunity to plead with the Deity, not to gratify the wishes of the impious dancers by leaving the place. The young converts caught up the cry put forth by the minister, that those who got up the ball were seeking to drive the Lord away from the village. So the prayer-meeting was pitted against the ball—the latter to drive the Lord away, the former to keep him there; and when it was known how signally the ball had failed, the remark was usually made, that the dancers had found the Lord too strong for them.

I doubt not that many who went into that revival, went into it from the same motive that leads people to a ball or a theatre—the love of excitement.

I knew I had been in a state of great excitement, and I knew not how much of the revolution in my mind, which was called conversion, was attributable to this. I obtained leave of Mr. B. to travel three weeks. I had a brother living in Pennsylvania, whom I wished to see. I turned my back on Norwich and the revival, which was then in full progress, and started off, on foot, to visit my brother. My motive for going was to get out of the excitement, and try how I should feel when I mingled with others who were not at all excited; I wanted to know if what I had experienced was to be any thing abiding.

I arrived in Pennsylvania, and had a pleasant time with my relatives. While there, my excitement cooled down in a good degree. Yet I felt no abatement of my determination to lead a religious life, as I understood that to mean.

I returned from Pennsylvania. The excitement had sub-sided greatly. The different churches were gathering in the new converts. That village I left in a strong convulsion; I found it calm. Meetings were continued, but no body seemed excited; all were engaged in their employments, as if nothing had happened.

Soon after my return, I "came forward," as it was called, to join the church. A meeting was to be held to examine candidates for admission to the Presbyterian Church. Over sixty came forward, myself among the rest. There I again told the story of my conversion, detailed the process through which I had passed, and which I honestly and sincerely thought was the great process through which all must pass to become Christians.

I was accepted with the rest, on condition of my declaration of belief in all the tenets put forth in the Westminster Catechism, which I then could honestly and truly make. The minister, elders, deacons and members were satisfied that I was a Christian, from the experience through which I had passed. I was, with the rest, formally propounded to be admitted; and a few Sundays after, we were all taken into the church.

Index

(Unless otherwise noted, all place names refer
to the State of New York.)

THE OLD GALLOWS

LEGAL HANGINGS IN GENESEE COUNTY, N.Y.
1807 - 1881

James MacClean   Age: Unknown
            Hanged: August 28, 1807

for axing to death his friend William Orr in a
dispute over a tree.

James Gray   Age: early 30's
            Hanged: November 5, 1830

for inflicting a fatal knife wound to tavern-
keeper, Samuel Davis during a barroon argument.

Indian William Smith   Age: Unknown

            Hanged: November 4, 1836

for the murder of the "Squaw of Etopkes Bighaus,"
however little more is known of the crime.

Benjamin David White   Age: 39
            Hanged: May 2, 1843

An athetist who shot to death his father, a
religious fanatic. Believing that athetism was
a worse crime than murder, many people felt that
the sentence should be commuted until White would
accept Christianity, then be hanged. White died
an athetist.

Levi Mayhew   Age: 23
            Hanged: May 5, 1866

for clubbing to death with a rock, Theodore Durham
in a dispute over Durham's wife, Sarah. Mayhew
was a Civil War veteran.

Thomas Quackenbush   Age: 27
                    Hanged: August 1 , 1876

for causing the death of Mrs. Sarah Norton by the
"effects of rape." Quackenbush "ravished," Mrs.
Norton in a way, "too disgusting to print," after
which she ran and hid in the outhouse, where she
caught pneumonia and died 2-3 weeks later.

Charles Stockley   Age: 24
                    Hanged: August 19, 1881

for shooting to death his employer, a farmer by the
name of Welker in a dispute over the farmer's
daughter who Stockley wanted to call upon. Stockley
was granted an insanity hearing one day before the
execution, but was found insane since his pulse and
respirations increased when discussing the hanging.
It is believed an insane person wouldn't know the
difference, therefore wouldn't care.

VICTIMS SENTENCED TO DIE BUT WHO ESCAPED THE GALLOWS:

Elijah Gray, father of James Gray, (hanged in 1830,)
was with his son when Samuel Davis was knifed. His
sentence was commuted to life imprisonment by plea
of his son. He served 7 years and then pardoned.

An Irishman named Currey, for killing another Irishman
named Faucett. Currey was declared insane and spent
the remained of his life in the lunatic asylum.

Polly Frisch, for the murder of her husband and three
of her children by the administration of arsenic. The
sentence was commuted to life imprisonment due to public
protest over hanging a woman. She spent one year in
prison, was declared hopelessly insane and sent to the
lunatic asylum. In 1892 she was pardoned by New York
Governer, Flowers.

INVITATION TO D. J. McPHERSON, PRESS REPRESENTATIVE,
TO BE PRESENT AT THE EXECUTION (by hanging) OF THOMAS
BURTON QUACKENBUSH, AUGUST 11, 1876.

PROCESSION

Sheriff and under-Sheriff
Clergy with prisoner
Physicians Tozier and Croff
Deputy Sheriffs
Reading of Death Warrant
Prayer
Goodbye
Pinion-place noose, cap
After taking body down inquest

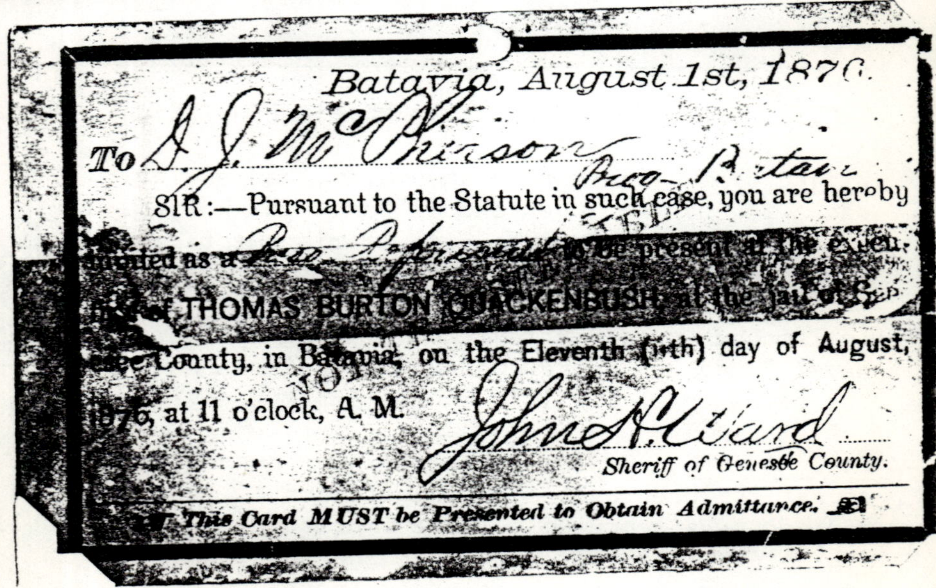

Batavia, August 1st, 1876.

To D. J. McPherson

SIR:—Pursuant to the Statute in such case, you are hereby invited as a Press Representative to be present at the execution of THOMAS BURTON QUACKENBUSH at the jail of Genesee County, in Batavia, on the Eleventh (11th) day of August, 1876, at 11 o'clock, A. M.

John H. Ward
Sheriff of Genesee County.

This Card MUST be Presented to Obtain Admittance.

INVITATION TO EXECUTION
BY HANGING AUG. 1. 1876.